Professions and Professionalism

Professions have long provided a dependable body of expertise that organisations have relied upon to fulfil goals. Issues around equality and diversity alongside challenges to expert knowledge in the neo-liberal era have created profound challenges for this type of worker, even while creating opportunities for newer varieties of expert labour to establish themselves as professionals.

This shortform book provides a critical synthesis of the current state of the field from an international perspective. It highlights the key opportunities and challenges for the professions and professionalism within both the public and private sectors as a field of research, practice and policy. The first half of the book deals with the comparative history, theories and inequalities of the professions. This provides a basis for our understanding of how the professions have had to adapt and how governance, management and leadership have come to shape the emerging and evolving models of professions and professionalism. The book draws on case studies and through its analysis illustrates the organisational and sociological dimensions of the field.

This book will be of interest to scholars, academics and students in the fields of business, management and sociology, especially those conducting research and studies around the professions and professionalism.

Mike Dent is Professor in the School of Justice, Security and Sustainability at Staffordshire University, UK.

State of the Art in Business Research
Series Editor: Geoffrey Wood

Recent advances in theory, methods and applied knowledge (alongside structural changes in the global economic ecosystem) have presented researchers with challenges in seeking to stay abreast of their fields and navigate new scholarly terrains.

State of the Art in Business Research presents shortform books which provide an expert map to guide readers through new and rapidly evolving areas of research. Each title will provide an overview of the area, a guide to the key literature and theories and time-saving summaries of how theory interacts with practice.

As a collection, these books provide a library of theoretical and conceptual insights, and exposure to novel research tools and applied knowledge, that aid and facilitate in defining the state of the art, as a foundation stone for a new generation of research.

Strategic Human Resource Management, 2e
A Research Overview
John Storey and Patrick M. Wright

Sales Management
A Research Overview
Kenneth Le Meunier-FitzHugh and Kieran Sheahan

Fundraising and Nonprofit Marketing, 2e
A Research Overview
Roger Bennett

Professions and Professionalism
A Research Overview
Mike Dent

For more information about this series, please visit: www.routledge.com/State-of-the-Art-in-Business-Research/book-series/START

Professions and Professionalism

A Research Overview

Mike Dent

Routledge
Taylor & Francis Group
LONDON AND NEW YORK

First published 2024
by Routledge
4 Park Square, Milton Park, Abingdon, Oxon OX14 4RN

and by Routledge
605 Third Avenue, New York, NY 10158

Routledge is an imprint of the Taylor & Francis Group, an informa business

British Library Cataloguing-in-Publication Data
A catalogue record for this book is available from the British Library

Library of Congress Cataloging-in-Publication Data
Names: Dent, Mike, 1944– author.
Title: Professions and professionalism: a research overview/ Mike Dent.
Description: Abingdon, Oxon; New York, NY: Routledge, 2024. | Series: State of the art in business research | Includes bibliographical references and index.
Identifiers: LCCN 2023028536 (print) | LCCN 2023028537 (ebook) | ISBN 9781138365216 (hardback) | ISBN 9781032619538 (paperback) | ISBN 9780429430831 (ebook)
Subjects: LCSH: Professions. | Professional employees.
Classification: LCC HD8038.A1 D46 2024 (print) | LCC HD8038.A1 (ebook) | DDC 331.7/1 – dc23/eng/20230629
LC record available at https://lccn.loc.gov/2023028536
LC ebook record available at https://lccn.loc.gov/2023028537

ISBN: 978-1-138-36521-6 (hbk)
ISBN: 978-1-032-61953-8 (pbk)
ISBN: 978-0-429-43083-1 (ebk)

DOI: 10.4324/9780429430831

Typeset in Times New Roman
by Apex CoVantage, LLC

For Madeleine Frances Tutt
1978–2021
In memory of her love, conversations and sense of fun

Contents

Acknowledgements

Back in 2016 the edited collection *The Routledge Companion to the Professions and Professionalism* was published, it was co-edited by me along with Ivy Lynn Bourgeault, Jean-Louis Denis and Ellen Kuhlman. This was the inspiration for this much shorter and more succinct volume although it is Terry Clague of Routledge I have to thank for suggesting that I actually write it. I owe him many thanks for his support and patience while awaiting the delivery of the finished manuscript. David Brock was very kind in providing access to *Journal of Professions and Organization* articles even before I was invited on to the advisory board. Sadly, many university libraries have limited access to the academic journals needed for research, and that includes my own. Other people who I must mention for their interest and help are Ian Kirkpatrick (University of York) and Geoff Heath (University of Keele) for providing useful and much-needed articles and an advanced copy of a very useful book. I would like to also thank Celia Davies and Hamish Main for our conversations around the professions while out walking in the Peak District. I am also indebted to all those discussions at the *International Sociological Association*'s conferences and congresses especially those within Working Group 52 (Professions and Professionalism) over recent years.

I have dedicated this book to Madeleine, my daughter, who sadly died of cancer during the writing of this book. She was an amazing and a much-loved person.

1 Professions and professionalism

Contemporary challenges

Introduction

The professions appear at times to be anachronistic, as institutions rooted in a past of occupational privilege and elitism. Picture, for example, the UK legal professionals in their wigs and gowns or university academics processing on awards days, it can all appear so very eighteenth century or even medieval. The professions can provide job security, high social status and a good income, the consequence often enough of their monopoly control – or jurisdiction – over a strategic segment of the division of labour. Certainly, the ceremonials associated with entering some professions have contributed to the sense of social inequalities. For example, to qualify as a barrister law graduates need to attend a dozen formal dinners at the Inns of Court (Aldridge 2011). The organised professions, however, have been seriously challenged over the last 50 years or so by the forces of neo-liberalism and have come under increasing public scrutiny. Throughout this book the term 'organised profession' will be used to refer to all those professions which are formally recognised by the state, whose members appear on a register and are obliged to comply to a code of good practice. These professions will be coordinated by their own association, which will act as a forum for the members as well as a mouthpiece for their interests. These professions will also oversee the education and training programmes for new entrants.

When comparing the professions across different Western countries, we can see marked differences in the way they are organised. This is particularly noticeable in the West when comparing Anglo-American and Continental European professions. In way of an illustration, there was a French TV police drama series, *Engrenages*, which in English was called 'The Spiral' which had been running for some years, and the final series was broadcast in the UK around the time I was completing the editing of a previous book on the professions (Dent, Bourgeault, Denis and Kuhlman 2016). The French legal profession – as well as the police – played a major role in the drama and whatever license had been taken in the service of dramatic storytelling, it clearly showed that the French legal system operates differently from its Anglo-American counterparts. The French legal system – and it is the case

DOI: 10.4324/9780429430831-1

across much of continental Europe – is based on the Napoleonic code (Krause 1996: 139; Pollitt and Bouckaert 2017) in contrast to the Anglo-American legal systems which are shaped by common law principles. Yet, even while the system and process of the two legal systems are distinctly different, one can still recognise professional commonalities. The work of advocates and magistrates in France, for example, corresponds broadly to that of barristers and judges in Britain and similarly to the attorneys and judges in the USA. By extension, we can also recognise the professions of medicine, nursing, teaching, journalism, computing and the military across different countries even though their history and organisation may be different. The reason will be partly isomorphic enabled in some regions by imperialism (see Chapter 3) where a country has gained a degree of regional or global hegemony, as in the cases of France and Britain in the past and, arguably, the USA today.

Challenges and risks

Despite the challenge of neo-liberalism, the professions have remained a significant force within the occupational ecology of all Western societies. This is in large part because of clients' twin concerns of trust and risk in relation to those crucial areas of human activity that brought them to the professional in the first place, typically relating to such matters as one's health, legal challenges or safety concerns over the building of bridges. This is a situation described by Giddens (1990) a few decades ago as 'riding the juggernaut' of late modernism and characterised by Beck (1992) as the 'risk society'. Within late modernity, Giddens (1990) argues that our engagement with the professional expertise (i.e. expert systems) is *disembedded.* It is removed from the immediacies of the here and now (ibid.: 28). We routinely trust the engineering embedded in the buildings, bridges, trains and cars we use. Similarly, to a large extent, for the legal, health and education systems. All are examples of *disembedding*. When we consult with specific professionals these abstract systems are, in Gidden's terms (ibid.: 88), *re-embedded* through the encounter (*facework*), and the effectiveness of the encounter (or ongoing encounters) will depend on the degree of trust there is in the professional and the expert systems she has access to. For example, the bridge won't collapse, one might be cured, you will succeed in your examinations and so on. Not only have the professions been intrinsically linked with trust, but they have also been closely associated with the control of uncertainty and risk. All this dates to the origins of the professions within the guilds of the late Middle Ages (Krause 1996), trust and the control of uncertainty have been the hallmarks of the professions. In attempting to minimise uncertainty professions provide practical advice and service to their clients typically through private and confidential means. In earlier times, these services were provided principally for aristocratic or royal patronage and later extended to the middle classes and subsequently mediated by the modern state. In European and later North American history the professions have been significantly shaped by the state, alongside the market and the universities (Burrage, Jarausch and Siegrist 1990) and – as Abbott 1988 has pointed out – other professions as well. The actual mix of influences within this actor network has varied between countries and regions as well as during different historical periods. All of this accounts for the differences between, for example, the English and French legal professions mentioned at the beginning of this chapter.

Significant in the formation of the professions in recent history was the rise of the Welfare State (e.g. Blomqvist and Winblad 2022) (see Chapter 2). This was reflected in the sociology of the professions in the shape of neo-Weberian social closure theory, which still enjoys considerable support within the academy (McDonald 1995; Saks and Adams 2019). The subsequent shift in social and economic policies towards neo-liberal approaches at the end of the twentieth century would appear to have undermined the social closure model of the professions. The newer neo-liberal approach to policy and organisations represented a threat to the organised professions and their strategies for social closure. Subsequently, we have seen significant reconfigurations across the professional field (Miller and Rose 2008: 79–82). In concrete terms, the most obvious neo-liberal impact took the form of New Public Management (NPM) (see Chapters 4 and 5). Initially, it was predominantly an Anglo-American phenomenon (Reed 2016: 202) but it also influenced much of Continental Europe, although a little less so in those countries with a legalistic 'Rechtsstaat' tradition, especially Germany (Pollitt and Bouckaert 2017; Kickert 2013: 97; Dent 2005). The Scandinavian countries, by contrast, were early and keen adopters of NPM (Hansen 2013). It was this radical disjunction (or shockwave) to the post-war settlement that had a major impact on public sector professionals.

The neo-liberal forces that gave rise to NPM also did much to reconfigure the work and organisation of professionals outside the public sector and facilitated the rise of the globalised professional services firms (Muzio, Aulakh and Kirkpatrick 2019) (see Chapters 4 and 5). So too with the freelance professionals occupying the interstitial spaces between the corporate and public sector worlds. In light of these developments it may have been better if we stopped using the term 'professions' and simply talked in terms of 'expert labour' or 'knowledge-based work' instead (see Chapter 2) (Muzio, Ackroyd and Chanlat 2008: 2; Gorman and Sandefur 2011). This would overcome some of the anachronism with the professions and professionalism, for example, the common assumption that the life of a professional is as part of a professional partnership (or solo practice). However, it is not as simple as that, for the discourse on the professions and professionalism has radically changed since the latter end of the twentieth century. Many experts today, for example, work in large corporate organisations where professionalism and managerialism are commonly hybridised into a distinct and often globalised variant of professionalism (Hinings 2016). Indeed, as Fournier (1999) pointed out a little while ago, we even have the widespread managerial practice of appealing to their staff to act with professionalism, even where there is no pretence that the occupation is a professional one at all. A perverse variant, perhaps, of 'bobilisation' (Gellner 1970) in which employees act with professionalism, but without the benefits of being a member of a profession. At the same time, within the professions, there has been a growth in a new generation of solo practice and small partnerships, for example, within computing and information technology. Yet here the practitioners are apparently less interested in the institutional aspects of professionalism; instead, their focus is solely on the market (Reed 1996). At the same time others, particularly therapists of various kinds working in the health sector, tend to be keen to claim institutionalised professional status, for example, in the cases of practitioners of complementary therapies (Fournier 2002; Saks 2015). The difference between the two is that the computing/IT specialist can make her professional reputation in the marketplace while the acupuncture practitioner or aromatherapist needs to establish her professional credentials and status not only to reassure potential clients but to be licensed to practice alongside more traditional health professionals (Saks 2015: 11). Professional status clearly retains its appeal within everyday discourse, even management is keen to be seen being a profession (Leicht 2016) despite managerialism often being seen as the nemesis of professionalism, with its priority of subsuming professionalism to business priorities. Perhaps, all things considered, it is useful to stay with the terminology of professions and professionalism, for these are the terms commonly used to make sense of expert labour. But we should do so only so long as we recognise that the professions are changing and changing in radical ways. In part, this is connected to the issue of professionalism, which might be defined as behaving in a responsible and trustworthy way in the best interest of the 'client'. It is the issue of trust that is a central one for the professions, but unlike previous assumptions (by both professionals and the public alike), it is no longer taken for granted (Brown and Calnan 2016). There is now a much more ambivalent attitude to the professions by both public and politicians. Professions are no longer assumed responsible enough to wholly self-regulate. Instead, professionals are now subject to a considerable degree of external regulation (see Chapter 4) (Dent 2018; Brown and Calnan 2016: 132–133).

Outline of chapters

The argument threaded through this short book is that the institutional arrangements that we think of as the professions are neither fixed nor rigid, although their adaption to new realities can often be difficult and awkward for those involved. Although, as we will see later, this is not always the case, for example, in the case of the growth of the globalised professional services firms (GPSF) (Flood 2011). Here law, accountancy and others have very quickly grasped the market opportunities of neo-liberalism to their advantage. Whether it is a case of challenges or opportunities, the professions are finding ways of adapting to survive and thrive in the twenty-first century but by means that radically reinterpret what the professions and professionalism have meant in the past.

In this short book there are four substantive chapters, bookended by this introductory chapter and a concluding discussion. Each substantive chapter deals with a distinct aspect of the professions and professionalism. The first two of these provide the basis for the latter two chapters, which deal with contemporary issues and challenges. Chapter 2 starts with a brief history of the professions before moving on to reviewing the changing theories of the professions and professionalism. One of the key features of the professions historically is the role they have played in reproducing inequalities of class, gender, race and ethnicity, which is the concern of Chapter 3. Chapter 4 moves onto the territory of professional regulation and governance and the dynamics of change over recent decades. This topic also entails an examination of the professions' relations with their clients/users/consumers as user involvement in its various guises is now an integral aspect of professional governance. There are strong links here with Chapter 5 which deals with the professions' relations with management and leadership and the issue of 'hybridity', that is, the extent to which professionals can also be effective managers. The concluding Chapter 6 provides an overview and reflection of the future of the professions.

References

All internet links accessed and checked on 24 May 2023 or later.

Abbott, A. (1988) *The System of Professions: An Essay on the Division of Expert Labor*. Chicago and London: The University of Chicago Press.

Aldridge, A. (2011) 'Barristers dinners–a bit of fun or one upper class indulgence too many?'. *The Guardian*, 12 May. Available at https://amp.theguardian.com/law/2011/may/12/barristers-dinners-fun-indulgence

Beck, U. (1992) *Risk Society: Towards a New Modernity*. London: Sage.

Blomqvist, P. and Winblad, U. (2022) 'Have the welfare professions lost autonomy? A comparative study of doctors and teachers'. *Journal of Social Policy*, 1–22, doi:10.1017/S0047279422000228.

Brown, P. and Calnan, M. (2016) 'Professional, trust and cooperation'. In M. Dent, I.L. Bourgeault, J.-L. Denis and E. Kuhlmann (eds) *The Routledge Companion to the Professions and Professionalism*. London: Routledge: 129–143.

Burrage, M., Jarausch, K. and Siegrist, H. (1990) 'An actor-based framework for the study of the professions'. In M. Burrage and R. Torstendahl (eds) *Professions in Theory and History*. London: Sage: 203–225.

Dent, M. (2005) 'Post new public management in public sector hospitals? The UK, Germany and Italy'. *Policy & Politics*, 33 (4): 623–636.

Dent, M. (2018) 'Health care governance, user involvement and medical regulation in Europe'. In J.M. Chamberlain, M. Dent and M. Saks (eds) *Professional Health Regulation in the Public Interest: International perspectives*. Bristol: Policy Press: 17–37.

Dent, M., Bourgeault, I.L. Denis, J.-L. and Kuhlmann, E. (2016) *The Routledge Companion to the Professions and Professionalism*. London: Routledge.

Flood, J. (2011) 'The re-landscaping of the legal profession: Large law firms and professional re-regulation'. *Current Sociology*, 59 (4): 507–529.

Fournier, V. (1999) 'The appeal of "professionalism" as a disciplinary mechanism'. *The Sociological Review*, 47 (2): 280–307.

Fournier, V. (2002) 'Amateurism, quackery and profession conduct: the constitution of "proper" aromatherapy practice'. In M. Dent and S. Whitehead (eds) *Managing Professional Identities: Knowledge, Performativity and the 'New' Professional*. London: Routledge: 116–137.

Gellner, E. (1970) 'Concepts and society'. In D. Emmett and A. MacIntyre (eds) *Sociological Theory and Philosophical Analysis*. London: Macmillan: 115–149.

Giddens, A. (1990) *The Consequences of Modernity*. Cambridge: Polity Press.

Gorman, E.H. and Sandefur, R.L. (2011) '"Golden Age," quiescence, and revival: How the sociology of professions became the study of knowledge-based work'. *Work and Occupations*, 38 (3): 275–302.

Hansen, H.F. (2013) 'NPM in Scandinavia'. In T. Christensen and P. Laegreid (eds) *The Ashgate Research Companion to New Public Management*. Farnham: Ashgate: 113–129.

Hinings, C.R. (2016) 'Restructuring professional organizations'. In M. Dent, I.L. Bourgeault, J.-L. Denis and E. Kuhlmann (eds) *The Routledge Companion to the Professions and Professionalism*. London: Routledge: 163–174.

Kickert, W.J.M. (2013) 'Public management reform in continental Europe: National distinctiveness'. In T. Christensen and P. Laegreid (eds) *The Ashgate Research Companion to New Public Management*. Farnham: Ashgate: 97–112.

Krause, E.A. (1996) *Death of the Guilds: Professions, States and the Advance of Capitalism, 1930 to the Present*. New Haven and London: Yale University Press.

Leicht, K.T. (2016) 'The professionalization of management'. In M. Dent, I.L. Bourgeault, J.-L. Denis and E. Kuhlmann (eds) *The Routledge Companion to the Professions and Professionalism*. London: Routledge: 188–199.

McDonald, K.M. (1995) *The Sociology of the Professions*. London: Sage.

Miller, P. and Rose, N. (2008) *Governing the Present: Administering Economic, Social and Personal Life*. Cambridge: Polity.

Muzio, D., Ackroyd, S. and Chanlat, J.-F. (2008) 'Introduction: Lawyers, Doctors and Business Consultants'. In D. Muzio, S. Ackroyd and J.-F. Chanlat (eds) *Redirections in the Study of Expert Labour*. Basingstoke: Palgrave: 1–28.

Muzio, D., Aulakh, S. and Kirkpatrick, I. (2019) 'Professional occupations and organizations'. In R. Greenwood and N. Philips (eds) *Elements of Organization Theory* (Cambridge e-book series). Cambridge: Cambridge University Press.

Pollitt, C. and Bouckaert, G. (2017) *Public Management Reform: A Comparative Analysis – Into the Age of Austerity*. Oxford: Oxford University Press.

Reed, M. (1996) 'Expert power and control in late modernity: An empirical review and theoretical synthesis'. *Organization Studies*, 17 (4): 573–597.

Reed, M. (2016) 'Leadership and "leaderism": The discourse of professional leadership and the practice of management control in public services'. In M. Dent, I.L. Bourgeault, J.-L. Denis and E. Kuhlmann (eds) *The Routledge Companion to the Professions and Professionalism*. London: Routledge: 200–214.

Saks, M. (2015) 'Inequalities, marginality and the professions'. *Current Sociology*, 63 (6): 850–868.

Saks, M. and Adams, T.L. (2019) 'Neo-Weberianism, professional formation and the state: Inside the black box'. *Professions & Professionalism*, 9 (2): 1–14. DOI.ORG/10.7577/pp.3190.

2 Origins and theories of professions

Introduction

In this chapter my purpose is twofold: first to provide a brief history of the professions within a comparative context and second, review the main sociological theories currently in play. The result of this historical and theoretical review, as will be seen, is how adaptable is the notion of a profession even if the institutional basis of professions appears so unchanging. The professions have rarely been dynamic institutions but faced with powerful external challenges they have proven to be adept at accommodating to most new realities. I will examine the ways professions have developed over the centuries and adapted more recently to the decline of the welfare state and the rise of neoliberalism over more recent decades.

A history of the professions

Historically, the professions have tended to be a conservative phenomenon; they have had protectionist aims and elitist intent. To achieve their aims aspiring professions would make claims (not always justified) to an expertise, a body of knowledge and ethical practice – and importantly, they will have nurtured an elite clientele. One can reflect, for example, on the history of medicine, where many therapies were ineffective and sometimes dangerous (e.g. Porter 1993) and the ethics of medical research in previous centuries have been highly dubious (Skloot 2010; Foucault 1973). Prior to the nineteenth-century professionalisation meant winning aristocratic and especially royal patronage. Here physicians and later surgeons had some success – although the dynamic was rather different as between the UK and continental Europe (Burrage and Torstendahl 1990; Abbott 1988). The Church and Law followed a different trajectory to that of medicine – but still dependent on royal sponsorship. For the cleric and lawyer, their success relied on their indispensability to the working of government in the development of European states (ibid.; Burrage and Torstendahl 1990). These three vocations were seen from early on as of elite status; Addison in 1711 wrote describing them as '[the]

DOI: 10.4324/9780429430831-2

three great professions of divinity, law and physic' (Carr-Saunders 1966: 3). While the Church has lost much of its cachet as a career choice, Law and Medicine have not, at least not yet and possibly not ever (Freidson 1994, 2001). All three originally gained their status from their relations with powerful aristocratic patrons and especially the state (Krause 1996; Macdonald 1995). Abbott (1988: 202) points out that a key difference between England and the USA, on the one hand, and Continental Europe on the other was that mainland European countries had state institutions in place, controlling and regulating professions much earlier than in the Anglophone countries. Consequently, professions seeking jurisdictional control, for example, in France would appeal directly to the state and welcomed regulation as evidence of professional legitimacy, which is different to the more market-mediated professions in the Anglo-American world (Abbott 1988: 158). On the whole, professionalism is associated with work within civil society, ideally aiding fellow citizens in their time of need and interceding on their behalf with the state. This was, broadly, Durkheim's view (1992), although one opposite to Shaw's (1987) much-quoted view that the 'professions are a conspiracy against the laity' which, despite predating by many decades, reflects the critical analyses of the professions in the 1970s and 1980s. Those focused on the professions' degree of control over their work and clients (Johnson 1972). These theoretical perspectives will be discussed later in this chapter.

The professions of law, medicine and divinity, known as the 'liberal' professions because they required a university degree, suggested that they had mastery of a complex knowledge base necessary for their vocation. They also enjoyed the status, autonomy and rewards that stemmed originally from aristocratic and state patronage. This, however, was not the only historical source of power for professions. Another strand that overlapped and intertwined in the history of the professions was that of the guilds (Krause 1996). From the Middle Ages the guilds were powerful institutions that oversaw the apprenticeship training and protected the 'mysteries' and status of the trades (ibid.: 3–9). It is from this quarter we find the other major source of professionalisation that emerged in the Middle Ages (ibid.: 4). Although it was rather later, in the eighteenth century, that the surgeons and apothecaries emerged from the guild system to become formally recognised and licensed as professions. In England of the eighteenth century, the medical professions were 'straightjacketed in its traditional, three-tiered, hierarchical structure' (Porter 1993: 34) with physicians at the top. But in practice and especially in the provinces, one would find the forerunners of general practice who needed to be physician, surgeon and apothecary all rolled into one – whatever their initial training was. Over time surgeons won an equal status with their physician colleagues, while apothecaries did not, at least not in the modern form of pharmacists. This was largely because their professional jurisdiction was subordinate to that of the physician. In the UK the formal professionalisation came about under Parliamentary Acts in the first quarter of the nineteenth century. This completed the process that separated them from their past as members of the Barber and Surgeons and the Apothecaries and Grocers guild.

Not all professions, however, emerged from the guild system; architects, for example, were something of an exception. They emerged from under aristocratic patronage to design fine buildings in the eighteenth century. In the UK, for example, architects were responsible for creating country houses that became popular among the aristocrats in that century. There were possibly as many as 840 designed and built, according to Bryson (2010: 206), across the English landscape. Architects as a formal profession with compulsory examinations did not happen until 1882 (ibid.: 216). In the USA architects professionalised a little earlier (Woods 1999: 4–5) but otherwise shared a similar course to their counterparts in the UK, although with less involvement of any landed aristocracy. Besides the construction of large houses there was also much interest in and patronage of science and technology, following the restoration of the monarchy in the previous century (Porter 2001a), which provided the historical basis for the establishment of science and engineering on their path towards professionalisation. Not that this development did anything at the time to undermine the pre-eminence of the Church, Law or Medicine.

There were several 'new' professions that came to the fore in the nineteenth century. Two notable examples would be Accountancy and Engineering, whose roots date back to the renaissance if not before (Carr-Saunders 1966), but as modern organised professions their rise was tied to that of industrial capitalism. The services they delivered were those needed by industry. Engineering institutions, from their beginnings, utilised their learned societies to both improve practice and status within each branch of engineering (Evetts and Jeffries 2005: 299). Like accountants, engineers tended to be employed within large industrial firms and benefitted from that patronage – and experiencing professionalisation more 'from above' than 'within' (Evetts 2003, 2013: 786). Equally, the standing of a professional firm would reflect the power and status of its principal clients, particularly given the localism of nineteenth-century practice (Johnson 1972: 69). The twentieth century witnessed a significant growth of public sector/human services professions with the expansion of the welfare state. Social Work and Nursing, as key examples, while having longer histories (e.g. Rogowski 2010; Turner 1995; Porter 1993), only now pursued their own professionalisation project (Larson 1977, 1997). Like the accountants and engineers before them, they too needed to gain state recognition achieved through licensing and registration. A similar path was followed in the USA coupled with the development of a specific knowledge base of 'social diagnosis' (Abbott 1988: 93).

One distinction between Accountancy and Engineering and the Human Services professions was that the first were largely based in the private sector while Nurses, Teachers and Social Workers were largely employed in the public sector. A second distinction has been gender, with many more women employed within Human Services than in engineering or accountancy. These were not in themselves factors for devaluing their professional status; nevertheless, they were labelled, contentiously, as *semi-professions* (Etzioni 1969; Nancarrow and Borthwick 2021: 108–109). Sociologically this is a baseless demotion, for at its simplest level the definition used to differentiate the professions was that of the discredited 'trait' approach (Johnson 1972). More crudely, it is evidence of the 'machismo theory of professionalisation' (Witz 1992: 61) based on the patriarchal assumption that female professionals are only equipped intellectually, organisationally or emotionally to work in a subordinate relationship to male professionals. However, there is another important reason for the power differences between the older and newer professions which relates to the limited ability of the newer heteronomous professions to gain total control over their jurisdictions (Abbott 1988: 71). This is partly because their jurisdiction is adjacent to and overlaps in places than of a more powerful profession (e.g. Medicine and Law) and partly because the state had, by the twentieth century, developed the ability to dictate the nature and extent of these professions jurisdictions. This was not quite analogous to the French *etatist* approach, yet still enough to limit the professional aspirations of these occupations. Larson's (1977, 1997) Weberian distinction between *autonomous* and *heteronomous* types is useful here. The older professions tended to have greater independence from the state, traditionally working within relatively small organisations that they effectively control. The relatively newer *heteronomous* professions (Nursing, Teaching, Social Work) tend to be employed within large state, or local state, bureaucracies. Their numbers grew with the growth of the welfare state and its need for a workforce with expertise working with people's problems and aspirations. Strauss, Fagerhaugh, Suczek and Wiener (1982) referred to this as *sentimental work* emphasising the professional's role in managing the patient's or client's journey to recovery or resolution. This is somewhat different from Hochschild's (1983) concept of *emotional labour* which is more concerned with the exploitative management of employees' presentation of self (e.g. Gray 2009; Isenbarger and Zembylas 2006; Kinman, Wray and Strange 2011; Winter et al. 2018). These *heteronomous* professions' workforces comprise a high proportion of females (see also Chapter 3 Inequalities), especially so in nursing, which led to an unjustified tendency to conflate human services work with the assumed natural and implicit skills of women and therefore discounted as knowledge and expertise. This contributed to such work being labelled 'semi-professional', as previously mentioned, which reflected the working of patriarchy within the professions (Witz 1992: 60–62; Falter 2015). During the latter part of the twentieth century these professionals were required to have university degree credentials. This was generally welcomed from within the professions as evidence of their elevation along the path of professionalisation. Similar developments have happened across the European community. Aina and Nicoletti (2018: 111) describe the process as one of becoming the same as the 'liberal professions', which etymologically equates these *heteronomous* professions with the *autonomous* ones. This, however, does not reflect their comparative jurisdictional capacities compared to the professions of law and medicine. Nevertheless, the working relationships between these professions are changing and they are no longer simply to be viewed in hierarchical terms.

During the latter twentieth century and beyond, especially in health and social care, other occupations working within the same division of labour also sought full, state-registered professional status. This group of occupations tended to be treated collectively, whether they were, for example, podiatrists/chiropodists, occupational or physio-therapists, or dental hygienists. Today, they are collectively referred to as the Allied Health Professions (Nancarrow and Borthwick 2021). These developments and parallel ones elsewhere on the professions landscape also reflect a shift from the 'heroic' individual professional to something closer to inter-professional teamwork. Although it is also true that some of these newer professions and professional specialities have emerged in competition with an established profession. For example, chiropody grew in the UK in face of opposition from the surgeons (Borthwick 2000). While, in other instances, it is the opposite, where one profession fills the gap left by another. As, for example, in the case of specialist nurses replacing doctors (Dent 2003: 105–107).

The ways in which these developments play out in different countries will vary, depending on a range of cultural, political and economic factors operating at the micro, meso and macro levels within society. Within new institutionalism (to be discussed later in this chapter) this is captured in the concept of path dependency. Moreover, as Wilsford (1994) has argued, while significant change is possible it is hard won and generally dependent on 'critical junctures', or 'punctuated equilibrium' (Tuohy 2018), those moments of crisis, or turbulence, including the accumulation of factors that together provide a 'tipping point' to change. This reality has shaped the history of the professions, particularly those working within the public sector. It accounts, for example, to the variation in the work organisation of the medical profession in the Netherlands, England and the USA (Tuohy 2018; Dent, Kirkpatrick and Neogy 2012). Yet despite the variations in the organisation of the professions internationally they can be recognised as sharing common characteristics. These relate to claims of skills and a knowledge base to justify an autonomy over the work processes, ethical practice and control of the programme of training and selection of new recruits. These claims have been the subject of some tension in recent times, much of it associated with the rise of neo-liberalism and with it New Public Management (NPM) (Hood 1991, 1995; Dent 2005), but before I turn to that discussion, it will be useful to more purposefully look at the historical development of the professions from within a broader European and North American perspective, with 'path dependency' firmly in mind.

The revolutionary disruption

The historical development of an institution such as a profession is sometimes thought of as incremental, as evolving through time. That is not always the case, within Europe and the USA, for example, the impact and aftermath of the French Revolutions (1789–1799) and the earlier American Revolutionary War (1745–1783) had significant influences on the way the professions evolved. The American Revolution ultimately led to a radical undermining of the professions, although not immediately so. Initially laws were enacted to retain the elite professions of law and medicine broadly along the lines of the British model. But by the Jacksonian Era dating from the 1840s this all changed. The politics of populism was associated with an antagonism towards the new capitalism and its 'privileged aristocracy of wealth' (Carroll and Noble 1988: 199). From then through to the end of the century, one no longer formally needed to gain qualifications in medicine or law – or any profession – anyone could practice and often did (Krause 1996: 30); the US citizenry valued the free market more than qualified professionals (Abbott 1988: 164). The federal structure of the USA itself deterred any attempts at establishing legal monopolies and jurisdictional boundaries. It was within this hostile reality that the professions re-organised themselves. National professional societies were created, with American Medical Association coming into being in 1848 and the Bar Association in 1868 (Krause 1996: 30). It was with the setting up of university-based professional programmes after 1865, however, that established the modern American professions – notably Medicine at John Hopkins and Law at Harvard (Krause 1996: 30). It was this that created the model of professional training that was to become the benchmark for the professions internationally.

The French Revolution was in many ways more radical than the American, for it effectively abolished organised professions – as corporations and guilds (Krause 1996: 130) – on the grounds they came between the state and the citizen. These professions were viewed as special interests that conflicted with the Rousseauian principle of the 'general will' (*volonté general*) and all universities and their medical schools were shut down and only reopened again under the Napoleonic State (Krause 1996: 131). Even then, under the Chapelier Law, no profession was permitted to organise independently of the state (Herzlich 1982: 245). The revolution replaced one strong state with another. There was little room for any civil society discourse based on 'interests'; professions had to use a different vocabulary, one based on defending their rights (*défendent leurs droit*) (Wilsford 1991: 34). While this rights-based professionalism is peculiarly French, it reflected the tensions between professions and the state elsewhere too. In England, the equivalent revolutionary moment was not so much the Civil War of the seventeenth century but the Industrial Revolution of the nineteenth century. This gave rise, eventually, to a stronger state and with it the construction of an effective system of public administration (Johnson 1972). This marked a shift from the classic *autonomous* professions to a more *heteronomous* professionalisation (i.e. subject to external regulations) (Larson 1977, 1979).

It was these revolutionary disruptions to the old order that ushered in the modern professions. Whilst many of them trace their past back to the guilds and corporations of medieval Europe, their success and viability lay in the new world of state licensing and accreditation. The relationship between profession and state, however, is never static (Light 1995) and by the latter end of the twentieth century it was the influence of neo-liberalism and, specifically, new public management (NPM) that came to dominate the public sectors in the UK, Scandinavia and Europe (Pollitt and Bouckaert 2017; Christensen and Per Laegreid 2011; Dent and Barry 2004; Dent 2003). NPM was initially seen as a solution to the economic challenges of the 1970s and 1980s and rested on assumptions of marketisation and consumerism being introduced into the public sector. This was thought to make the sector and the associated professions more efficient and accountable (Leicht 2016: 195–196) by the state imposing external controls on the work of the professions. Despite NPM's failure to achieve its goals (ibid. 2016: 196) and the evidence that it is in decline (Pollitt and Bouckaert 2017: 212), there has been no return to the *status quo ante*. All of this suggests that the professions have an ambiguous relationship with the state as well as with their work organisations as reflected, for example, in Foucault's discourse of governmentality and disciplinary power (Foucault 1979; Martin, Myles Minion, Willars and Dixon-Wood 2013; Evetts 2003; Johnson 1995) discussed further in Chapter 4. Now, however, it is time to move on to the discussion of contemporary theory.

Part 2: organisational and sociological theories of the professions

There are, at least, two strands dominant in the study of the professions: the sociological and the organisational. They are not independent of each other, with sociology having a longer history of involvement in the subject (Evetts 2013). However, today, organisational studies provide a significant forum for much of the research and debate (e.g. see *Journal of Profession and Organisation*). Probably the key text here is Powell and DiMaggio's *The New Institutionalism in Organizational Analysis* (1991), which brought together organisational analysis and sociological theory within an institutional approach (including the study of professional work). In the introduction, DiMaggio and Powell (1991) dated the birth of *new* institutionalism to Meyer and Rowan's (1977) paper, which is included in the 1991 volume (Powell and DiMaggio 1991: 41–62). This paper argued that formal organisational structures can be best understood as 'myth and ceremony' and emphasised the socially constructed nature of organisational reality (Berger and Luckman (1967). DiMaggio and Powell (1991: 22–26) also set out their indebtedness to sociology more generally, which includes Garfinkel, Giddens, Goffman, Collins and Bourdieu. The importance of this sociologically oriented approach to organisational analysis is its role in shaping organisational thinking on the professions (Muzio, Brock and Suddaby 2013).

The older institutionalists (e.g. Selznick 1966; Gouldner 1954) had argued that organisations were 'based on their values and leadership . . . [further] shaped by interaction with community members' (Jennings and Greenwood 2003: 197). While new institutionalists agree with this position, they fundamentally reconstituted it. Jennings and Greenwood (2003: 197) summarised the changes as follows:

> (1) reframe[ing] the concepts and language of old institutionalism . . . (2) specif[ying] the mechanisms of change more precisely, (3) connect[ing] organization-level processes to processes at more macro and micro levels and (4) consider[ing] the possibilities of sedimentation and deinstitutionalization.

To clarify a couple of these terms: 'sedimentation' is where a newer archetype is layered on top of a pre-existing one. One example would be where the newer corporate management archetype overlays the collegiate professionalism to which university academics, for example, remain wedded. A similar example would be the response of hospital doctors to similar processes at work in the field of health care (e.g. Dent, Kirkpatrick and Neogy 2012: 117–118; Kitchener 1999). The implication is that the professionals, or a subset of these, will lack commitment to the newer archetype and may actively work against it. The other challenge is that of 'deinstitutionalisation' which, according to Oliver (1992), may be the consequence of political, functional or social pressures. These are hastened or slowed by the degree of organisational entropy or inertia in play. In the case of the professions, the process of deinstitutionalisation implies de-professionalisation, although in practice – as will be discussed in Chapter 5 – the pressure on professions has led to adaptations, which have reconfigured their professionalism, rather than significantly eroding their status.

New institutionalism is particularly concerned with change and DiMaggio and Powell (1991: 67–74) provide an influential typology of isomorphism: (1) *coercive*, (2) *mimetic* and (3) *normative* to account for the variation in causes of change. It is the third of these that has the most direct relevance to the professions for it concerns the way professions respond to such pressures so as to find an optimum way to try and maintain their occupational autonomy. These result from discussions within the profession (and with others, including state actors) over time. One example would be the way in which the English medical profession came to accept quite radical changes in governance practices in the wake of the introduction of new public management policies and related reforms (Dent 2003). Although in that case the profession was subjected to the full range of *isomorphic* pressures. *Coercively* as this relates to government legislation and regulations (to force a compliant response), plus a strong strand of the *mimetic* in the mix too, for by emulating practices adopted elsewhere (that appeared to be effective) is perceived as a relatively low-risk strategy to take. It is even more enlightening to compare how the English doctors adapted to that of their European colleagues (ibid., Dent, Kirkpatrick and Neogy 2012).

New institutionalism provides an effective means to analyse professions and professional work. Two books that illustrate this well are Brock, Powell and Hinings (1999) and Scott, Ruef, Mendel and Caronna (2000). The first, *Restructuring the Professional Organization*, covers accounting, health care and law. Here we find the application of Hinings and colleagues' concept of archetypes (combining interpretative schema, system and structure [Hining, Greenwood and Cooper 1999: 132–135]). These, they argue, develop within the 'fields' of interdependent organisations; they are configurations that are well adapted to prevailing expectations and requirements for legitimacy. The model was originally developed in connection with accountancy and has since been extended to the broader grouping of expertise within the professional service firm (Hinings 2016) as well as to health care (Kitchener 1999; Dent, Howorth, Mueller and Preuschoft 2004). In Scott, Ruef, Mendel and Caronna (2000), another similar but different framework is proposed that 'provide[s] coherence, meaning and stability to a field' (Scott, Ruef, Mendel and Caronna 2000: 20). This is three-part model comprising (1) institutional logics; (2) institutional actors; and (3) governance systems. Here institutional logics further need elaboration, for it has become a crucial aspect of the new institutionalism. Institutional logics provide the organising principles for a field (Friedland and Alford 1991). They are the basis of taken-for-granted rules guiding the behaviour of field-level actors and they 'refer to the belief systems and related practices that predominate in an organizational field' (Scott 2001: 139). Logics are an important theoretical construct because they help to explain connections that create a sense of common purpose and unity within an organisational field (ibid.).

Logics appear to have a *prima facie* correspondence to organisational culture, but there seems to be little crossover between the two. Hinings (2012: 99) suggests that, whereas organisational culture tends to assume (or aspire to) a unified culture, institutionalists are happy to work with the notion that organisations can hold several logics at the same time without them necessarily being in conflict (Reay and Hinings 2009; Lounsbury 2007). This, however, does not preclude one logic from becoming dominant and in the process being fundamental to the conceptualisation of institutional change (Reay and Hinings 2009). As for example the changing logics of professional work in the face of new public management (Laihonen and Kokko 2020; Lingard, Oswald and Le 2019; Berg and Pinheiro 2016). Compare this to the approach of sociologists.

Segue to sociology

Here the influence of Weber (Saks 2016a; Saks and Adams 2019) is very apparent, even more pronounced than within neo-institutionalism. This is the consequence of the success of the neo-Weberian approach that came to dominate the study of the professions, especially from the 1970s onwards. This approach was highly critical of the trait and functionalist accounts of the professions that had dominated the field in the 1950s on the grounds of those theorists' uncritical analyses of the professions' own sense of self-worth. The functionalist analysis grew out of Durkheim's assumption that the professions would continue to contribute positively to advanced industrial societies in acting with social responsibility and altruism (Ackroyd 2016: 16–17). Professions were seen as key actors in civic society in challenging the state in the interests of their clients. While Durkheim's analysis did not necessarily imply that the professions would automatically contribute to social order, only that they would *improve* its functionality. But when these ideas were taken up by Parsons (1953) the assumed functionality of the professions in the maintenance of the social order changed from being a possibility to being a certainty, an essential element in maintaining the homeostasis of society (Ackroyd 2016: 17).

To put the neo-Weberian approach in its own historical context, it grows out of a fierce debate about the middle classes in Late Capitalism (Macdonald 1995; Dent 1993; Saks 2016a). For the neo-Weberian, the middle-class assets of knowledge and credentials are what is utilised to secure social closure and usurpation (see Macdonald 1995: 55–56). In the case of the professions, effective social closure strategies have depended on the particular character of the state (and therefore the degree of autonomy and self-governance the profession could achieve) and capitalist development. Two works are particularly relevant here, Johnson's (1972) *Professions and Power* and Larson's (1977) *The Rise of Professionalism*, both distinguished between *autonomous* and *heteronomous* professions (although Johnson does not use these terms, his typology matches this distinction). The first (*autonomous*) refers to the liberal professions and the latter to those employed within work organisations (*heteronomous*). Interestingly and importantly, both authors went on to engage with Marxian and Foucauldian theory to extend their analyses of the professions (to be discussed later in the chapter). More recently, Evetts (2013: 11) has adopted a similar distinction between 'organizational' and 'occupational' professionalism, observing that while the 'organizational' variety is rooted in Weberian models of organisation, the 'occupational' variety owes more to Durkheim's model of occupations as moral communities standing between the state and the individual. While professions based on collegial authority may constitute moral communities, it does not mean necessarily that they do not seek to protect and/or advance their jurisdictions. In other words, one should never assume that professions are entirely philanthropic.

Theories do not grow in a historical vacuum and neo-Weberian accounts of the professions reflected the changing realities of professional work across the Western world in the 1960s and 1970s. Here they enjoyed an unchallenged ascendance within the occupational order, largely because of their key role within the welfare state. The post-war settlement of the late 1940s and

1950s had effectively placed public sector professionals in charge of running health, education and social care (e.g. Dent 2003; Kirkpatrick, Ackroyd and Walker 2005). Medicine, for example, was able to claim a dominant, largely autonomous, jurisdiction and while the influence of teachers, social workers and nurses was more constrained, reflecting a heteronomous jurisdiction; they, nevertheless, largely shaped the services they delivered. There was much debate in the 1970s and 1980s around the potential 'proletarianization' or 'corporatization' of these professions (Oppenheimer 1973; Derber 1982; McKinlay and Arches 1985; McKinlay and Stoeckle 1988; Freidson 1994, 2001: 129–132) and Marxian analysts theorised in terms of the ambivalent class position (or 'contradictory class locations') of the professions as part of the new middle class; as 'global capitalist' or 'collective labourer' (Dent 1993; Abercrombie and Urry 1983). The non-Marxists were more interested in the concept of the service class (Goldthorpe 1982), which turned out to be lacking in homogeneity, more concerned to pursue their own group interests and generally limited in the degree in which they functioned (to use a Gramscian term popular at the time) as 'organic intellectuals' of the capitalist class (Dent 1993: 251).

The sociology of professions, according to Abbott (2001 cited in Sciulli 2008: 5), is 'a branch of the sociology of work concerned with the analysis of expert occupations'. Larson too adopted a similar viewpoint although her emphasis has been more on the 'construction and social consequences of expert knowledge' (Larson 1990: 25). This marked a move away from a Weberian approach and, for Larson, one towards a Foucauldian perspective. Important here, if a bit technical, is her preference for Foucault's notion of 'discursive field' over Bourdieu's 'scientific field' (Larson 1990: 33–34) because it is more inclusive. Whereas the scientific field is somewhat institutionally bounded, the discursive field is not. This is, for Larson, particularly helpful in the analysis of expert labour – including professional work. For example, she distinguishes between managerial and professional discourses and how these produce different 'truths' (ibid.: 38) for they are a matter of 'authorization and power' (ibid.: 37), which varies between these two groups (managers and professionals). But it is important to note that professional discourses are not limited to professionals, for as Fournier (1999) has shown others also employ these discourses (see also Fournier 2002). Fournier (1999) argues that professionalism as discourse is also utilised as a form of work discipline ('action at a distance') this is referred to as 'responsibilisation' (ibid. 1999: 291). This extends well beyond members of organised professions, to include middle-managers, administrative and sales staff – and many others too. The idea is that staff are 'empowered' to discipline themselves to work efficiently in serving their clients/customers and in the best interests of their employers. This is 'responsibilisation', which for Fournier (1999), is an aspect of governmentality (Foucault 1979). By extension, from a Foucauldian perspective, professional autonomy is predicated on governmentality or as Miller and Rose (2008: 34) phrase it, 'government at a distance'. Doctors manage sickness and legitimate absenteeism from work; lawyers, peoples' expectations of the legal system; teachers, the expectation of young people (as well as preparing them for the labour market) and so on. To quote Johnson (1995: 11):

> From a Foucauldian perspective a history of the professions becomes one part of the transformation of power associated with governmentality. . . . The rapid crystallization of expertise and the establishment of professional associations in the nineteenth century was directly linked to the problems of governmentality – including the classification and surveillance of populations, the normalization of the subject-citizens and the discipline of the aberrant subject.

This reflected a shift in state power, from claims to sovereign power to one of popular legitimacy (Johnson 1995: 10), or disciplinary power (Clegg 1989: 155). For Foucault, power is exercised *within* the society, not from *above* it (Foucault 1981: 95–96). This is not to assume that the professions are simply acting like a specialist police directly under the direction of the state; it is more nuanced, reflecting shifting network of alliances (ibid.: 95–96). This perspective provides a useful analysis of the shifting relations between (and within) professions, their work organisations, clients and the state. It also can be used alongside Actor–Network Theory (ANT) (Dent 2003: 37–38; Clegg 1989: 202–203), which Scandinavian institutionalists have done with good effect (Czarniawska and Sevón 1996; Clegg 2010: 9).

For the neo-Weberian, there is much in a Foucauldian approach to critique, largely based on its high level of abstraction which would seem to deny any detailed empirical study, such as that from an interactionist perspective (Macdonald 1995: 25–26). In the same vein, the notion of governmentality, in its merging of the professions into the state (Johnson 1995), makes the latter appear monolithic and all-encompassing (Saks 2016a: 174). This criticism ignores Foucault's concept of the discursive field (mentioned earlier), especially in connection to power and its inherent instability within alliances and networks. Another related criticism of Foucault and governmentality more generally has been the overlooking of the importance of 'agency' (Martin and Waring 2018) and for showing little 'sensitivity to diversity, heterogeneity and resistance' (Bevir 2011a: 462). However, recently new translations of his lectures at the Collège de France offer a different Foucauldian perspective of 'agency' one based on Foucault's notion of 'pastoral power' (Martin and Waring 2018; Waring and Latif 2017), which has been interpreted as a 'descriptive metaphor for "expert power"' (Waring and Latif 2017: 1070). Martin and Waring (2018: 8) argue that health professionals, especially doctors, 'advise and counsel' their patients, who are autonomous subjects who may not simply and passively comply.

The critique of Foucault's work on the grounds that it is too abstract and not readily applicable to empirical research (Saks 2016b: 75) is also undermined by his notion of pastoral care. Interestingly, it has strong parallels with Weber's (1963) earlier analysis of 'a priesthood . . . exercise[ing] long term domination over laity' (Eyal 2013: 875) through pastoral ministering. Eyal (2013) argues that this is also an important component of a Foucauldian analysis of expert (including professional) power. This power and expertise, however, is grounded in networks and reflects a process of 'co-production', which includes the patients/clients (Eyal 2013: 875–876). Pastoral power is clearly not limited to the liberal professions (i.e. those that have been able to provide themselves with a firm shelter from the vagaries of the labour market [Freidson 1994: 80–84]). Others working as organisational (or heteronomous) professionals can possess it, for example, nurses, allied health professions and social workers.

As already has been mentioned, it has been argued that we should move away from using the category of 'professions' and use 'expert labour' instead (Muzio, Ackroyd and Chanlat 2008: 1–2). Here the literature is even more firmly grounded within organisational and critical management studies more than sociology *per se*, even if the analysis itself is solidly sociological. It is useful here to note Reed's (1996: 575) clarification of the terms used:

> the expertise of . . . expert [labour] must be storable, controllable, indeterminable . . . and protectable if it is to be a reasonably stable cognitive and social base for the institutionalization of expert power.

For it also encapsulates the assumed essentials of a profession. Such an approach, however, allows for the inclusion of other occupational groups not formally recognised as professions. One key example is the professional services firms (PSFs), which are 'the largest, most complex and globally diversified organizations in the contemporary economy' (Muzio, Aulakh and Kirkpatrick 2019: 1), but they are not solely or predominantly comprised of members of organised professions. These organisations grew out of accounting and law firms (i.e. employing accredited professionals) but now extend to business consultancy, more generally, along with computer and information specialists. Within these ranks are occupations that have been pursuing professional projects, including human resource (HR) specialists (Suddaby and Viale 2011: 431). But the main factor distinguishing them from the established *autonomous* (independent) and *heteronomous* (organisational) professionals is that PSFs' power strategy is based on marketisation as opposed to social closure (monopolisation) or credentialism (Reed 1996: 586). This is so even where the knowledge/expert workers employed within the PSFs are themselves members of organised professions.

An occupational grouping to be found both within and outside PSFs are the computer and informational specialists. They have their national professional bodies to which they may belong, although many of these experts do not take up membership as registration is not mandatory (Dent 1996: 20). This group of cognate occupations straddles the line between employment within PSFs and entrepreneurial practice. This is a group of entrepreneurial professions, or knowledge workers, that has grown with the rise of neo-liberalism from 1980 onwards and who depend on 'a highly esoteric and intangible knowledge base' (Reed 1996: 595) to maintain – and extend – their autonomy and jurisdiction. Their relevance here is that they are exemplars of a more discursive notion of professions and professionalism, one in which the clients/users and public more generally identify these specialists as professional whether they are members of an organised profession or not. Here it is their assumed expertise and knowledge coupled with their performativity that establishes them as professionals.

This newer world of professions and professionalism is one that de-emphasises (but does not remove) the ambition of those pursuing a professionalisation project (Larson 1977: 66–80; Macdonald 1995: 55–61; Freidson 1994: 80–84). Instead, the emphasis is more a performative one where an occupation can advance its professional identity by its ability to validate its claim to an expertise based on and/or validated by scientific knowledge and for which there is a real market demand (Dent and Whitehead 2002: 8). This performative – as opposed to regulative – approach to professionalisation has been a relatively successful one for a range of newer occupations from management consultants to alternative therapists.

Conclusion

In this chapter the main strands of the history of the professions have been presented albeit on a broad canvas. This has shown up the plasticity of the concept of the professions, given that the notion of a profession has varied by historical period, as has the relative roles of the state and the market. Mainland European and Scandinavian professions have been much more shaped by their close relations to the state than has been the case in the English-speaking world. The focus of this chapter has been solely on developments in the West. This has meant that the colonial history of the professions in Africa and Asia and the implications for race and ethnic inequalities have been left out. This was not my intention, but for the reason of space, it has not been possible to include the subject in the chapter. I will, however, deal with the issues of race and ethnicity in the next chapter (*Professional Inequalities*). It was equally impossible, given the limits of space available, to present a definitive review of the organisational and sociological theories of professions and professionalism. Instead, I have largely concentrated on the main approaches and debates that currently dominate the literature.

References

All internet links accessed and checked on 24 May 2023 or later.

Abbott, A. (1988) *The System of Professions: An Essay on the Division of Expert Labor*. Chicago and London: The University of Chicago Press.

Abbott, A. (2001) 'Sociology of professions'. In N.J. Smelser and P.B. Bates (eds) *International Encyclopedia of the Social and Behavioural Sciences*. Amsterdam and New York: Elsevier Science.

Abercrombie, N. and Urry, J. (1983) *Capital, Labour and the Middle Classes*. London: George Allen & Unwin.

Ackroyd, S. (2016) 'Sociological and organisational theories'. In M. Dent, I. Bourgeault, J.-L. Denis and E. Kuhlmann (eds) *The Routledge Companion to the Professions and Professionalism*. London: Routledge: 15–30.

Aina, C. and Nicoletti, C. (2018) 'The intergenerational transmission of liberal professions'. *Labour Economics*, 51: 108–120.

Berg, L.N. and Pinheiro, R. (2016) 'Handling different institutional logics in the public sector: comparing management in Norwegian universities and hospitals'. *Research in the Sociology of Organizations*, 45: 145–168.

Berger, P.L. and Luckman, T. (1967) *The Social Construction of Reality*. Harmondsworth: Penguin.

Bevir, M. (2011a) 'Governance and governmentality after neoliberalism'. *Policy & Politics*, 39 (4): 457–471.

Borthwick, A. (2000) 'Notes and issues: Challenging medicine: The case of podiatric surgery'. *Work, Employment & Society*, 14 (2): 369–383.

Brock, D., Powell, M. and Hinings, C. R. (eds) (1999) *Restructuring the Professional Organization: Accounting, Healthcare and Law*. London and New York: Routledge.

Bryson, B. (2010) *At Home: A Short History of Private Life*. London: Transworld/Black Swan.

Burrage, M. and Torstendahl, R. (1990) *Professions in Theory and History*. London: Sage.

Carroll, P.N. and Noble, D.W. (1988) *The Free and the Unfree: A New History of the United States* (2nd edition). Harmondsworth: Penguin/Pelican.

Carr-Saunders, A.M. (1966) 'Professions: their organization and place in society'. In H.M. Vollmer and D.L. Mills (eds) *Professionalization*. Eaglewood Cliffs, NJ: Prentice-Hall: 3–9.

Christensen, T. and Laegreid, P. (2011) *The Ashgate Research Companion to New Public Management*. Farnham: Ashgate.

Clegg, S. (1989) *Frameworks of Power*. London: Sage.

Clegg, S. (2010) 'The state, power and agency: Missing in action in institutional theory?'. *Journal of Management Inquiry*, 35: 202–225.

Czarniawska, B. and Sevón, G. (1996) *Translating organizational change*. Berlin: Walter de Gruyter.

Dent, M. (1993) 'Professionalism, educated labour and the state: Hospital medicine and the new managerialism'. *Sociological Review*, 41 (2): 244–273.

Dent, M. (1996) *Professions, Information Technology and Management in Hospitals*. Aldershot: Avebury.

Dent, M. (2003) *Remodelling Hospitals and Health Professions in Europe: Medicine, Nursing and the State*. Basingstoke: Palgrave.

Dent, M. (2005) 'Post new public management in public sector hospitals? The UK, Germany and Italy'. *Policy & Politics*, 33 (4): 623–636.

Dent, M. and Barry, J. (2004) 'New public management and the professions in the UK: Reconfiguring control?'. In M. Dent, J. Chandler and J. Barry (eds) *Questioning the New Public Management*. Aldershot: Ashgate: 7–20.

Dent, M., Howorth, C., Mueller, F. and Preuschoft, C. (2004) 'Archetype transition in the German health service? The attempted modernisation of hospitals in a north German state'. *Public Administration*, 82 (3): 727–742.

Dent, M., Kirkpatrick, I. and Neogy, I. (2012) 'Medical leadership and management reform in hospitals: a comparative study. In C. Teelken, E. Ferlie and M. Dent (eds) *Leadership in the Public Sector: Promises and Pitfalls*. London: Routledge: 105–125.

Dent, M. and Whitehead. S. (2002) 'Configuring the "new professional"'. In M. Dent and S. Whitehead (eds) *Managing Professional Identities: Knowledge, Performativity and the 'New' Professional*. London: Routledge: 1–16.

Derber, C. (ed) (1982) *Professionals as Workers: Mental Labor in Advanced Capitalism*. Boston: G.K. Hall.

DiMaggio, P. and Powell, W.W. (1991) 'The iron cage revisited: institutional isomorphism and collective rationality in organizational fields'. In W.W. Powell and P. DiMaggio (eds) *The New Institutionalism in Organizational Analysis*. Chicago and London: University of Chicago Press: 63–82.

Durkheim, E. (1992) *Professional Ethics and Civil Morals* (2nd edition). London: Routledge.

Etzioni, A. (ed) (1969) *The Semi-Professions and Their Organization: Teachers, Nurses, Social Workers*. London: Collier-Macmillan.

Evetts, J. (2003) 'The sociological analysis of professionalism: Occupational change in the modern world'. *International Sociology*, 18 (20): 395–415.

Evetts, J. (2013) 'Professionalism: Values and ideology'. *Current Sociology*, 61 (5–6): 778–796.

Evetts, J. and Jeffries, D. (2005) 'The engineering and science institutions in the UK: changes, ambiguities and current challenges'. *European Journal of Engineering Education*, 30 (3): 299–308, doi: 10.1080/03043790500114425.

Eyal, G. (2013) 'For a sociology of expertise: The social origins of the autism epidemic'. *American Journal of Sociology*, 118 (4): 863–907.

Falter, F.M. (2015) 'Threatening the patriarchy: Teaching as performance'. *Gender and Education*, 1 (28): 20–36, doi: 10.1080/09540253.2015.1103838.

Foucault, M. (1973) *The Birth of the Clinic*. London: Tavistock.

Foucault, M. (1979) 'On governmentality'. *Ideology & Consciousness*, 6: 5–22.

Foucault, M. (1981) *The History of Sexuality: Volume One – An Introduction*. Harmondsworth: Pelican/Penguin.

Fournier, V. (1999) 'The appeal of "professionalism" as a disciplinary mechanism'. *The Sociological Review*, 47 (2): 280–307.

Fournier, V. (2002) 'Amateurism, quackery and profession conduct: The constitution of "proper" aromatherapy practice'. In M. Dent and S. Whitehead (eds) *Managing Professional Identities: Knowledge, Performativity and the 'New' Professional*. London: Routledge: 116–137.

Freidson, E. (1994) *Professionalism Reborn: Theory, Prophecy and Policy*. Cambridge: Policy.

Freidson, E. (2001) *Professionalism: The Third Logic*. Cambridge: Polity Press.

Friedland, R. and Alford, R.R. (1991) 'Bringing society back in: Symbols, practices and institutional contradictions'. In W.W. Powell and P.J. DiMaggio (eds) *The New Institutionalism in Organizational Analysis*. Chicago and London: University of Chicago Press: 232–263.

Goldthorpe, J.H. (1982) 'On the service class, its formation and future'. In A. Giddens and G. McKenzie (eds) *Social Class and the Division of Labour*. Cambridge: Cambridge University Press: 162–185.

Gouldner, A.W. (1954) *Patterns of Industrial Bureaucracy*. Glencoe, IL: Free Press.

Gray, B. (2009) 'The emotional labour of nursing–defining and managing emotions in nursing work'. *Nursing Education Today*, 29 (2): 168–175.

Herzlich, C. (1982) 'The evolution of relations between French physicians and the state from 1880 to 1980'. *Sociology of Health and Illness*, 4 (3): 241–253.

Hinings, B. (2012) 'Connections between institutional logics and organizational culture'. *Journal of Management Inquiry*, 21 (1): 98–101.

Hinings, C.R. (2016) 'Restructuring professional organizations'. In M. Dent, I.L. Bourgeault, J.-L. Denis and E. Kuhlmann (eds) *The Routledge Companion to the Professions and Professionalism*. London: Routledge: 163–174.

Hinings, C.R., Greenwood, R. and Cooper, D. (1999) 'The dynamics of change in large accounting firms'. In D. Brock, M. Powell, and C.R. Hinings (eds) *Restructuring the Professional Organization: Accounting, Healthcare and Law*. London and New York: Routledge: 131–153.

Hochschild, A.R. (1983) *The Managed Heart: Commercialization of Human Feeling*. Berkeley, LA and London: University of California Press.

Hood, C. (1991) 'A public management for all seasons'. *Public Administration*, 69 (1): 3–19.

Hood, C. (1995) 'The "new public management" in the 1980s: Variations on a theme'. *Accounting, Organizations and Society*, 20 (2/3): 93–109.

Isenbarger, L. and Zembylas, M. (2006) 'The emotional labour of caring in teaching'. *Teaching and Teacher Education*, 22 (1): 120–134.

Jennings, P.D. and Greenwood, R. (2003) 'Constructing the iron cage: Institutional theory and enactment'. In R. Westwood and S. Clegg (eds) *Debating Organization: Point-Counterpoint in Organization Studies*. Oxford: Blackwell: 195–207.

Johnson, T. (1972) *Professions and Power*. London: Macmillan.

Johnson, T. (1995) 'Governmentality and the institutionalization of expertise'. In T. Johnson, G. Larkin and M. Saks (eds) *Health Professions and the State in Europe*. London: Routledge: 7–24.

Kinman, G., Wray, S. and Strange, C. (2011) 'Emotional labour, burnout and job satisfaction in UK teachers: The role of workplace social support'. *Educational Psychology*, 31 (7): 843–856.

Kirkpatrick, I., Ackroyd, S. and Walker, R. (2005) *The New Managerialism and Public Sector Professionalism*. Basingstoke: Palgrave Macmillan.

Kitchener, M. (1999) '"All fur and no knickers": Contemporary organizational change in United Kingdom hospitals'. In D. Brock, M. Powell and C.R. Hinings (eds) *Restructuring the Professional Organization: Accounting, Healthcare and Law*. London and New York: Routledge.

Krause, E.A. (1996) *Death of the Guilds: Professions, States and the Advance of Capitalism, 1930 to the Present*. New Haven and London: Yale University Press.

Laihonen, H. and Kokko, P. (2020) 'Knowledge management and hybridity of institutional logics in public sector'. *Knowledge Management, Research and Practice*, doi: 10.1080/14778238.2020.1788429.

Larson, M.S. (1977) *The Rise of Professionalism: A Sociological Analysis*. Berkeley, LA and London: University of California Press.

Larson, M.S. (1990) 'In the matter of experts and professionals, or how impossible it is to leave nothing unsaid'. In R. Torstendahl and M. Burrage (eds) *The Formation of Professions: Knowledge, State and Strategy*. London: Sage: 24–50.

Larson, M.S. (1997) 'Professionalism: Rise and fall'. *International Journal of Health Services*, 9 (4): 607–627.
Leicht, K.T. (2016) 'The professionalization of management'. In M. Dent, I.L. Bourgeault, J.-L. Denis and E. Kuhlmann (eds) *The Routledge Companion to the Professions and Professionalism*. London: Routledge: 188–199.
Light, D. (1995) 'Countervailing powers: A framework for professions in transition'. In T. Johnson, G. Larkin and M. Saks (eds) *Health Professions and the State in Europe*. London: Routledge: 25–41.
Lingard, H., Oswald, D., and Le, T. (2019) 'Embedding occupational health and safety in the procurement and management of infrastructure projects: Institutional logics at play in the context of new public management'. *Construction Management and Economics*, 37 (10): 567–583.
Lounsbury, M. (2007) 'A tale of two cities: competing logics and practice variations in the professionalizing of mutual funds'. *Academy of Management Journal*, 50: 289–307.
Macdonald, K.M (1995) *The Sociology of the Professions*. London: Sage.
Martin, G., Myles, L., Minion, J., Willars, J. and Dixon-Wood, M. (2013) 'Between surveillance and subjectification: The developing governance of quality and safety in English hospitals'. *Social Science & Medicine*, 99: 80–88.
Martin, G.P. and Waring, J. (2018) 'Realising governmentality: Pastoral power, governmental discourse and the (re)constitution of subjectivities'. *The Sociological Review*, 66 (6): 1292–1308.
McKinlay, J.B. and Arches, J. (1985) 'Towards the proletarianization of physicians'. *International Journal of Health Studies*, 15: 161–195.
McKinlay, J.B. and Stoeckle, J.D. (1988) 'Corporatization and the social transformation of doctoring'. *International Journal of Health Studies*, 18: 191–205.
Meyer, J.W. and Rowan, B. (1977) 'Institutionalized organizations: formal structure as myth and ceremony'. *American Journal of Sociology*, 83 (2): 340–363.
Miller, P. and Rose, N. (2008) *Governing the Present: Administering Economic, Social and Personal Life*. Cambridge: Polity.
Muzio, D., Ackroyd, S., and Chanlat, J.-F. (2008) 'Introduction: Lawyers, doctors and business consultants'. In D. Muzio, S. Ackroyd and J-F. Chanlat (eds) *Redirections in the Study of Expert Labour*. Basingstoke: Palgrave: 1–28.
Muzio, D., Aulakh, S. and Kirkpatrick, I. (2019) 'Professional occupations and organizations'. In R. Greenwood and N. Philips (eds) *Elements of Organization Theory* (Cambridge e-book series). Cambridge: Cambridge University Press.
Muzio, D., Brock, D. M., and Suddaby, R. (2013) 'Professions and institutional change: Towards an institutionalist sociology of the professions'. *Journal of Management Studies*, 50: 699–721.
Nancarrow, S. and Borthwick, A. (2021) *The Allied Health Professions: A Sociological Perspective*. Bristol: Policy Press.
Oliver, C. (1992) 'The antecedents of deinstitutionalization'. *Organization Studies*, 13 (4): 563–588.
Oppenheimer, M. (1973) 'The proletarianization of the professional'. In P. Halmos (ed) *Professionalization and Social Change* (Sociological Review Monograph 20). Keele: Keele University Press: 213–127.
Parsons, T. (1953) *The Social System*. Glencoe, IL: The Free Press.
Pollitt, C. and Bouckaert, G. (2017) *Public Management Reform: A Comparative Analysis – into the Age of Austerity*. Oxford: Oxford University Press.

Porter, R. (1993) *Disease, Medicine and Society in England, 1550–1860* (2nd edition). Cambridge: Cambridge University Press.

Porter, R. (2001a) *Enlightenment: Britain and the Creation of the Modern World*. Harmondsworth: Penguin.

Powell, W.W. and DiMaggio, P.J. (1991) *The New Institutionalism in Organizational Analysis*. Chicago and London: The University of Chicago Press.

Reay, T. and Hinings, C.R. (2009) 'Managing the rivalry of competing institutional logics'. *Organizational Studies*, 30 (6): 629–652.

Reed, M. (1996) 'Expert power and control in late modernity: An empirical review and theoretical synthesis'. *Organization Studies*, 17 (4): 573–597.

Rogowski, S. (2010) *Social Work: The Rise and Fall of a Profession?* Bristol: Policy Press.

Saks, M. (2016a) 'A review of theories of professions, organizations and society: The case for neo-Weberianism, neo-institutionalism and eclectism'. *Journal of Professions and Organization*, 3: 170–187.

Saks, M. (2016b) 'Professions and power: A review of theories of professions and power'. In M. Dent, I. Bourgeault, J.-L. Denis and E. Kuhlmann (eds) *The Routledge Companion to the Professions and Professionalism*. London: Routledge: 71–85.

Saks, M. and Adams, T.L. (2019) 'Neo-Weberianism, professional formation and the state: Inside the black box'. *Professions & Professionalism*, 9 (2): 1–14. DOI. ORG/10.7577/pp.3190.

Sciulli, D. (2008) 'Revisionism in sociology of professions today: Conceptual approaches by Larson'. *Sociologica*, 3: 1–55, doi: 10.2383/28765.

Scott, W.R. (2001) *Institutions and Organizations* (2nd edition). London: Sage.

Scott, W.R., Ruef, M., Mendel, P.J. and Caronna, C.A. (2000) *Institutional Change and Healthcare Organizations: From Professional Dominance to Managed Care*. Chicago and London: The University of Chicago Press.

Selznick, P. (1966) *TVA and the Grass Roots*. New York: Harper & Row.

Shaw, G.B. (1987) *The Doctor's Dilemma*. Harmondsworth: Penguin.

Skloot, R. (2010) *The Immortal Life of Henrietta Lacks*. London: Macmillan.

Strauss, A., Fagerhaugh, S., Suczek, B. and Wiener, C. (1982) 'Sentimental work in the technologized hospital'. *Sociology of Health & Illness*, 4 (3): 257–278.

Suddaby, R. and Viale, T. (2011) 'Professionals and field-level change: institutional work and the professional project'. *Current Sociology*, 59 (4): 423–442.

Tuohy, C.H. (2018) *Remaking Policy: Scale, Pace, and Political Strategy in Health Care Reform*. Toronto and London: University of Toronto Press.

Turner, B.S. (1995) *Medical Power and Social Knowledge* (revised edition). London: Sage.

Waring, J. and Latif, A. (2017) 'Of shepherds, sheep and sheepdogs? Governing the adherent self through complementary and competing "pastorates"'. *Sociology*, 52 (5): 1069–1086.

Weber, M. (1963) *The Sociology of Religion*. Boston: Beacon Press.

Wilsford, D. (1991) *Doctors and the State: The Politics of Health Care in France and the US*. Durham and London: Duke University Press.

Wilsford, D. (1994) 'Path dependency, or why history makes it difficult but not impossible to reform health care systems in a big way'. *Journal of Public Policy*, 14 (3): 251–283.

Winter, K., Morrison, F., Cree, V., Hadfield, M., Ruch, G., and Hallett, S. (2018) 'Emotional labour in social workers' encounters with children and their families'. *British Journal of Social Work*, 49 (2): 168–175.

Witz, A. (1992) *Professions and Patriarchy*. London: Routledge.

Woods, M.N. (1999) *From Craft to Profession: The Practice of Architecture in Nineteenth Century America*. London: University of California Press.

3 Professional inequalities

Introduction

Back in the mid-twentieth century social class would have been identified as the main inequality endemic within the professions. More recently, however, a longer list has been identified that includes principally gender, race and ethnicity – and diversity more generally, including members of the Lesbian, Gay, Bisexual, Trans and Queer/Questioning (LGBTQ+) community and their intersectionality. These are issues of particular importance to our understanding of the professions because they have become something of a litmus test in assessing whether there has been any real transformation of the professions which mark a significant decline in the institutionalised patriarchy that traditionally characterised the professions (Hearn 1982; Witz 1992; Davies 1996). The professions and particularly the long-established ones of Law and Medicine were constructed on the principle of exceptionalism. They believe themselves to be different from, and – in their specialist fields – better than others. In certain important respects this is justified, entrants to these organised professions must undergo training programmes and submit to a degree of regulation that, in theory, ensures their expertise is effective, useful and (more recently) open to a degree of scrutiny. Historically, in order to establish their claims to providing the best care available the medical profession pursued a policy of delegitimating the work of charlatans and quacks. This, however, was a little disingenuous for medical science at that time (circa eighteenth century) was far from a reliable basis for diagnosis or treatment (Porter 2001b). Instead, the argument was more about restricting the medical market to themselves. That is not to say some charlatans and quacks were (and are) not peddling dangerous remedies, only that the professions were possibly more interested in protecting their interests than those of their patients. This would also have been part of the thinking behind the collective social mobility projects that characterised the organised professions in the nineteenth and especially twentieth centuries (Macdonald 1995). By the second half of the nineteenth century, professional status was increasingly based on educational qualification and professional training, ratified by state registration.

DOI: 10.4324/9780429430831-3

In principle this emphasis on educational qualifications could have led to an entirely meritocratic system, completely independent of any issues of gender, race and ethnicity, or class. But this was never the reality, for the established professions were primarily intent on pursuing strategies of exclusion to maintain their monopoly jurisdiction over crucial activities within society. With the extension of the role of the state in the twentieth century, particularly with the establishment of the Welfare State (Esping-Andersen 1990; Hill 2013), there was a further growth of the professions, this time particularly in teaching, nursing (as well as allied health professionals) and social work. Now, however, the State played a greater role in the organisation and regulation of these professions than had previously been the case with the established professions (Macdonald 1995). Moreover, these 'new' professions were characterised by the large number of women recruited into their ranks. This gendered reality has been critical in the dynamics of the jurisdictional politics of inter-professional and state relations. This has had direct implications for social status and income for the various organised occupational groups (Witz 1992). Yet, gender is only part of the story (Hearn, Biese, Choroszewiszewicz and Husu 2016), the dominance within the professions of white, middle-class men is also related to issues of race, ethnicity, class and the LGBT+ communities; moreover, these cannot be understood in isolation to one another. As feminist research has shown (McCall 2005) we need to better understand the intersectionality dynamics for the professions and professional identity.

While it has been feminist research that has brought the issue of intersectionality to the fore in the study of the profession it will have been post-colonial studies among other related influences that have raised the profile of race and ethnicity within the professions. In our post-colonial world, the dynamics of inequality within the professions have changed complex ways. Globally, professions have opened up opportunities within some settings, such as within certain parts of the legal profession in India (e.g. Ballakrishnen 2016) but have also been seen as a site for ongoing racial and gender inequalities in others as in the case of South Africa (Bonnin and Ruggunan 2016). These examples are discussed further within this chapter.

This chapter examines the extent to which these inequalities continue to shape the professions and whether they have been eradicated along with the dominance of white metropolitan males. These issues will be analysed in terms of their intersectionality as well as their implications for professional identity and careers.

Intersectionality, inequalities and professional identity

It may seem complicated trying to understand how individual and collective differences in relation to gender, along with the other signifiers of the inequitable inequalities, that include race, ethnicity and class, and complexly interrelate with one another (i.e. intersectionality); nevertheless, it is important to try (Hearn and Husu 2011; Elliot, Earl and Maher 2017). Among other considerations these interrelations also interconnect with professional identity. Without an analysis of these interrelations one can arrive at specious conclusions as to the relative inclusiveness and equality of the professions. For example, current data for several countries shows that the number of women entering the medical profession continues to rise (GMC 2020; Eurostat 2018; Association of American Medical Colleges [AAMC] 2018). *If* this means *only* an increase in white middle-class females entering medicine, then the inclusiveness of the profession would only be *marginally* improved. Meanwhile, evidence suggests that overall white males continue to predominate in senior positions. In the case of the UK, Milner, Baker, Jeraj and Butt (2020: 6) report that the 'NHS continues to favour white candidates and male candidates, for the most prestigious and best compensated positions'. Clearly, in the medical profession inequalities still prevail. Up until at least the latter decades of the twentieth century the whole notion of the professions and professionalism was distinctly patriarchal (Hearn 1982; Witz 1992; Davies 1996), and to an extent this, arguably, remains the case even now. Professions that appear to contradict this assertion, because their membership is predominantly female, still find themselves 'labelled' as 'lesser' or 'semi-' professions (Etzioni 1969; Hearn 1982; Davies 1996; Bolton and Muzio 2008) and their governance arrangements constrained, providing less occupational autonomy as compared to the established professions. Classic examples would be nursing (Abbott 1988: 71–72), teaching (Bolton and Muzio 2008: 8–10) and social work (Dent 2017: 26–27). The fact that these professions have historically enjoyed less autonomy than, for example, law and medicine, does not make them 'semi-professions' (see Chapter 2). It is worth noting, however, that the traditional autonomies of the established professions are currently also being eroded – as will be discussed further in Chapter 4. This may imply a convergence of sorts but, in jurisdictional terms, it probably does not. This is in part because the occupational jurisdictions, for example, of the professions of nursing and social work, are dominated by that of another profession (e.g. nursing and medicine). There are other differences including lack of theoretical knowledge and reliance of a third party (the state) for clients that have been argued undermine these professions claim to full professional status (Katz 1969; Witz 1992: 60–62). But on closer examination these characteristics are of less significance than have been claimed. Much of the established professionals' work, for example, is provided by the state or large corporate organisations (e.g. doctors working in public health services, corporate lawyers), both implying a monopsonist relationship. Moreover, much of a professional's work, whether in law or social work (as examples), is now designed to follow detailed practical guidelines or pathways (see Chapters 4 and 5). Also, one needs to remember, all these organised occupations, whether assumed to be 'semi-professions' or 'full' professions, are formally and legally established as professions. It may well be very useful to distinguish them in terms of whether they are 'organisational/heteronomous' or 'occupational/autonomous' types of professions (Evetts 2011; Larson 1977), but not in terms of whether they are wholly or partly a profession. There are examples in certain European countries, in the case of nursing, where the occupation has not been formally recognised as a profession – or not until very recently (Dent 2003). In Italy, for example, the professions are formally organised into *ordini* which regulate themselves and advise government and this makes them a profession (Dent 2002), Italian nursing, however, was until recently, not formally a profession, being organised as a *collegi* a lower status form of organisation. Nursing was only recognised as a profession in 2018 when it was finally 'promoted' to *ordini* status (FNOPI 2021). A parallel situation exists in Germany (Dent 2002) where nursing lacks the legal rights and obligations of other professions, as they are not permitted to organise as professional chambers, unlike doctors (*artzkammern*). To a large extent the lack of formal professional recognition has not been in line with the reality of professional organisation and training that exists within these countries.

The caring professions of nursing and social work emerged in their modern form later than other organised professions (e.g. accountancy, engineering). Their work has been predominantly within the public sector and their numbers made up largely of women (particularly so in nursing). Moreover, they have been unable to negotiate as strong an autonomy from the state as those other professions who established their formal status in the nineteenth century (Witz 1992). This is connected to the fact that they have not been able to establish as robust a jurisdiction as other more established professions working in their field. It partly derives from the role of state mediation (Johnson 1972), partly from patriarchy and partly because of the ethos of practical caring among practitioners (rather than any esoteric knowledge) (Macdonald 1995: 133–138). These caring professions, as indicated earlier, have been identified as being governed by heteronomous principles (Larson 1977: 68), reliant on state registration and licensure as well as for the state to provide the practitioners with patients and clients. To understand the relatively lower status and power of these professions it is necessary to understand the patriarchal nature of modern professions (Witz 1992) and that *historically* full professionalisation could only come about if it was completely monopolised by men (Hearn 1982: 195–196). The situation today is becoming more complex, as the professions generally pronounce a commitment to gender equality and are actively recruiting increasing number of women into their ranks, while – paradoxically – still evidencing gendered values and processes (Hearn, Biese, Choroszewicz, and Husu 2016: 59). It is the predominantly patriarchal nature of female employment that has dictated that care work including nursing and social work is largely female work.

One outcome of these professions being labelled as 'semi-professions' (Etzioni 1969) has led nursing to continue to pursue professionalisation strategies, despite already being formally a profession. One aspect of continued nursing professionalisation would be the increased specialisation within nursing and the taking on of tasks previously the responsibility of doctors (Dent 2003: 104–107). In the UK this professionalisation strategy has been as much a consequence of the state's willingness – and expectation – for nurses to take on these specialist responsibilities as it has been for the nursing profession pursuing the policy on its own account (Dent 2008: 110–113). Extending nursing roles would in all probability be a less expensive alternative for the state than employing more doctors. Nursing, in the English-speaking world, has, consequently, largely followed this specialisation route, leading to the introduction of nurse consultants and specialist nurses. This has typically come about because of a shortage of doctors in that area of activity or area, for example, in rural health care in the USA and Australia. Similarly, in Sweden and other Scandinavian countries (Dent 2003). This is, however, less elsewhere in mainland Europe, for example, in Germany (Dent 2002) and in the Netherlands. Here the debate is ambivalent as to whether nursing should reflect an emphasis on care or specialisation (van Schothorst-van Roekel, Weggelaar-Jansen, de Bont and Wallenburg 2020). The latter point has also been reflected within UK debates although not to the extent that nurse specialisation was significantly slowed or halted (Dent 2008: 11). Despite strategies to upgrade these professions and exorcise patriarchy from the workplace the relative devaluation of so-called 'women's' as opposed to 'men's' work will probably continue and distort any analysis of occupational vocation and expertise. There is, however, some evidence that the influence of patriarchy is waning under the pressure of managerialism, as will be discussed later in this chapter.

The issues of race and ethnicity in terms of professional recruitment and career have had a different dynamic and will be discussed further later in the chapter but it is important to point out here that it impacts gender and *vice versa* and similarly with class too (e.g. Acker 2006). Race and ethnicity issues have intra-professional effects often coupled with global implications, relating to migration and colonial/post-colonial tensions. In the metropolitan countries, 'professional mobilities', that is migration, has over many years provided a flexible workforce, although one that is 'highly gendered, classed and "racialized"' (Bourgeault, Wrede, Benoit and Neiterman 2016: 296). This also raises the very real issue of a professional brain drain from their countries of origin (Pang, Langsang and Haines 2002; Misau, Al-Sadat and Gerei 2010; Botezat and Ramos 2020). Although in some cases, professional mobility is to be viewed as part of a country's exports as in the classic case of the Philippines where nurses are trained in the expectation of their migrating to the USA, Saudi Arabia and UK and various other countries (Lorenzo, Galvez-Tan, Icamina and Javier 2007: 1411; Smith and Gillin 2021). These migrating nurses then support the Philippines economy by sending money back to their families.

In terms of social class, a topic to be returned to later in this chapter, professions are formally identified as middle-class occupations (Savage et al. 2013) and traditionally the more established professions have tended to be resistant to working-class recruitment. Gatekeeping would be by recruiting only from specific universities and colleges and further reinforced by the high economic entry costs. Examples would include internships, and once you have qualified, having the resources to buy into a partnership or practice (Macdonald 1995: 57). The dynamics of these subtle class inequalities are still evident today even among newer professions, including Information Technology specialists as Giazitzouglu and Muzio (2021) have recently demonstrated, and in ways that intersect with masculinity too.

Finally, for this section, we need to consider the LGBT+ community and their members' experience of working within the professions. Recent evidence suggests that lesbians and gays commonly experience workplace inequality coupled with stigma within the professions. Westwood's (2022) international literature review reports on religious-based negativity towards LGBTQ persons within social work, social and health care professions. But while Westwood (2022) identifies the negativity her review is unable to identify the implications for professional work or recruitment into these professions. Other studies have shown that LGBTQ+ identity for professionals is often experienced as a stigmatised one. Stenger and Roulet's (2018) study of French auditors reported that the majority of homosexual auditors concealed their sexuality from their colleagues and clients for fear of being misjudged. This reflects Cech's (2022) study of LGBTQ+ professionals working at NASA in the USA. Although here the evidence is perhaps less negative as they were able to build up trust and credibility over time and experienced little or no negativity (or stigma). However, where the work was organised into dynamic project-based teams and one had to establish trust and credibility 'heteronormative, hegemonically masculine interactional norms' prevailed (Cech 2022: 190). The systemic implications for inequalities at least for LGBTQ+ professionals working within the science, technology and mathematics (STEM) sector within the USA has been reported by Cech and Waidzunas (2021). They report that LGBTQ+ persons are more likely to 'report limited career opportunities and to have their professional expertise devalued by colleagues' (Cech 2021: 5). Clearly, gays and lesbians and no doubt others within the LGBTQ+ community can experience a disjunction between their personal and professional identities and one which for some, possibly most, is translated into an experience of inequality within their professional lives.

Professional identity and managerialism

Professional identity develops throughout the aspiring professional's education and training; this creation of a neophyte identity is one of proto-professionalism (Dent 2017: 29; Hilton and Slotnick 2005), a process of individual professionalisation, of adopting and identifying with the role, or the discourse of being a professional. The new professional that has emerged in the wake of the impact of managerialism (see Chapter 5) has tended to be rather different to what one might think of as the classic or established variety. The white middle-class male, heroic and individualistic (whether, for example, in the courtroom or in the hospital operation theatre), assumed to be completely trustworthy, very knowledgeable and highly skilled. This is an idealised version of the classic model, but one that the neophyte may well still aspire and, with it, its implicit patriarchal elements (Hearn 1982; Hearn, Biese, Choroszewicz and Husu 2016: 62–63). This masculinist model is one that has become increasingly anachronistic as the growing complexity of much legal and medical work has meant a greater emphasis of teamwork both intra- and inter-professionally. In addition, the impact of globalisation and marketisation on the professions, in the public and private sectors, have played their part in eroding these patriarchal elements from the professional identity. Now the professional has typically been transformed into the 'practitioner' who is:

> Flexible [and], reflective . . ., the team worker, lifelong learner, a person concerned to constantly update their knowledge and skills base, to be market-orientated, managerial, even entrepreneurial.
>
> (Dent and Whitehead 2002: 3)

This represents a decline in the individualistic professionalism that characterised the patriarchal professional model. It also marks a shift in many areas of professional work more towards managerial and regulated models of organisation (see Chapters 4 and 5). This development does not of itself ensure the end to male dominance, but it does make it easier for these organisations to be regulated regarding their policies relating to diversity, inclusivity and intersectionality generally. These developments, as it happens, also offer greater opportunities for flexible working arrangements in contrast to the previous 'heroic' and individualistic model of professionalism. This means, for example, there is a better prospect – if not always the reality – of work-life balance even for those with hands-on family responsibilities (Crompton and Lynette 2011; Boiarintseva and Richardson 2019). In sum, there is now the expectation that the professions will consist of women as well as men on a basis of full equality.

The entry of women in many professions is beginning to reach a similar percentage to that for men (Sommerlad and Ashley 2015), although less so in senior positions. For instance, in the UK the Financial Reporting Council (FRC) (2021) tells us that women make up just over 50% of managers within audit firms, but only around 33% of the directors and 18% become partners (FRC 2021: Figure 40: 49). Women are, however, more likely to achieve a senior management position within firms with less than 200 employees than within the larger firms (FRC 2021: Figure 41: 50). In the USA, within Accountancy more generally, the trend is similar (although these figures are not directly comparable; nevertheless, they do illustrate the overall situation). For example, in 2019 within firms employing more than 100 accountants (i.e. CPAs: Certified Public Accountants) women made up 45–46% of managers and 45% of directors/non-equity partners (AICPA 2021: 5). Whereas, in firms with less than 10 CPAs the figures are higher with females comprising 71% senior managers, 66% managers and 51% directors/non-equity partners.

The figures for race and ethnicity diversity in the USA are substantially lower. The demographics of new accounting graduates and masters in 2018 stood at only 30% for all people of colour (i.e. 'other than white' groups) of which only 4% were Black/African American and 14% for those of Asian/Pacific Islander heritage (AICPA 2019: 20). There has been virtually no change over the last decade (AICPA 2019: 21).

The gender figures are broadly similar for the legal profession, with women in England and Wales making up 49% of solicitors in private practice in 2020 (Law Society 2020). By contrast, only just over 18% of women in private practice are partners as compared to 40% of men (ibid.). On the other hand, women make up 68% of the solicitors working in central and local government, which would suggest there are barriers to women finding employment within the larger firms within private practice (ibid.). Barristers, that other branch of lawyers within the English and Welsh legal system, include an even lower proportion of women within their ranks. As of December 2020, the figure was 38.2%, a rise of only 0.2% in December 2019 (Bar Standards Board 2021: 3). In the USA, the figures for the legal profession are similar. At the associates level, for example, the National Association of Women Lawyers (NAWL) 2020 survey reported that women constitute nearly 47% of associates in private law firms. The figures for partners, however, are rather better in comparison to England and Wales at 31% for non-equity partners and 21% for equity partners, although these figures are much less than half that of their male colleagues (69% and 79%, respectively) (National Association of Women Lawyers 2021: 5).

In that other established profession, medicine, female doctors now make up 48% of the England and Wales workforce, as compared to Scotland where the figure currently stands at 53% (General Medical Council 2019: 3). The proportion of women entering medical school (i.e. joining the medical register) in 2019 stood at 54%, which represents, perhaps surprisingly, a decline of 4% since 2012 (General Medical Council 2019: 3). In the USA female enrolment is rising and stood at 49.5% for the 2018–2019 intake, while male enrolment is slowly declining (AAMC 2018: Table B3). It is not so easy to access the data for student enrolment across the EU, but Eurostat (2018) does tell us that in 2016 women made up 49% of the medical workforce, which is slightly higher than that for the USA (AAMC 2018: Table B3–B4). Clearly, the make-up of most professions, including law and medicine, is more diverse than 20 years ago. Nevertheless, women still tend to find themselves clustered in the lower-grade and paid positions, a consequence of 'feminization . . . fuel[ing] patterns of gender exclusion, stratification, and segmentation' (Bolton and

Muzio 2008: 283). As an illustration, in 2019, 52% of solicitors in England and Wales were women, but only 31% in private practice are partners (The Law Society 2020: 7–8). Moreover, the proportion of female partners drops even further amongst the more elite firms where the percentage shrinks to less than 10% (Sommerlad and Ashley 2015).

Intersectionality: inequalities of ethnicity, race and gender

The case of Law in the UK is an interesting one, in that currently their Black, Asian and Minority Ethnic members represent 17% of all solicitors, those of Asian descent are the largest group at 10% (as compared to 7% of the working population) (The Law Society 2020: 15, Table 7). The issues of inequalities relating to race and ethnicity tend to have a different dynamic to that of gender, despite parallels because of certain commonalities due to the structure of dominance and oppression across societies (Nagel 2003). There is, however, much more of a sense of 'otherness' at play with 'race' and 'ethnicity' (Neiterman and Bourgeault 2015: 617; Nagel 2003). The 'Other' derives from Simmel's category of the 'Stranger' (Simmel 1971: 144) for it provides the rationale for defining the boundaries to 'otherness' – real or symbolic (Kastoryano 2010: 79). In the case of the professions, given their historic patriarchal assumptions (Macdonald 1995; Witz 1992) these boundaries, culturally, subordinated all persons other than older white males. In addition to women (as well as younger men), this included non-white persons. This last category is largely the consequence of the West's history of colonialism and slavery (Fuchs 2018). Moreover, the particularities of their experiences have had left different traces within the various post-colonial countries as well as having different implications for those in North America, Europe and Australasia. To compare two historical examples, that of medicine in West Africa and law in India, at least as presented by Patton (1996) and Dezalay and Garth (2010). For West African doctors, their experience was of having 'to contend with a lower status in the professional ranks' (Patton 1996: 15) even though they trained alongside Europeans and felt themselves equal to their English counterparts. All of this led to intra-professional conflict between African doctors, their white British counterparts and the Colonial Medical Service. However, other than withdrawing from the Colonial Medical Service altogether and entering private practice (which would pay rather less than the Colonial Medical Service), there was little that the African doctor could achieve. The Indian lawyers' experience of working with British colonialism was, on the other hand, rather different, although it too was hugely affected by racism. 'Law came with colonialism' (Dezalay and Garth 2010: 4) and the colonial powers needed to co-opt local elites to underpin their claim to legitimacy. This elite was drawn from the Brahmins. Membership of the legal profession provided the social and cultural capital for the young men of these local elites and provided their main route to political power. They became in the nineteenth century 'an aristocracy of compradors' and in the twentieth, the leaders of the nationalist movement (Dezalay and Garth 2010: 66–67). These histories have in various ways informed the development of the professions within post-colonial societies. Bonnin and Ruggunan (2016), for example, provide an illustrative case study of race and gender inequalities within the professions, consequent on the transition to post-apartheid South Africa. Under apartheid people of colour were allowed to enter the professions (as were women) but only under very restricted terms. They could only attend racially designated universities, and there were disproportionally more universities open to white students than to the African, Indian and 'coloured' (i.e. people of colour). Then, when they qualified, they were with very few exceptions only allowed to practice in the townships and homelands away from white citizens. Public sector professionals were more accessible and perhaps had greater autonomy, whether they were doctors, nurses, social workers or teachers. But only to practice in non-white areas, 'black hands' on 'white bodies' was seen as an anathema (Bonnin and Ruggunan 2016: 253). Post-apartheid, the South African state has adopted a twin-prong strategy of widening access for both non-white citizens and all women to all the professions. Even so, there is still evidence of racialised patterns of recruitment and promotion within the professions (e.g. law and accountancy) despite the legislated de-racialisation of the professions (Bonnin and Ruggunan 2016: 253–254). Moreover, the official policies appear to impact more on the professionalisation of the public sector, where this translates into greater 'professional' certification of managerial work, skills and competency training along with a rhetoric of professional status. This would appear to be impacting more on improving the quality and efficacy of public service delivery than necessarily expanding access to the professions for people of colour and women.

The Indian case, as already indicated, has been somewhat different. First, the professions and professionalism had been accessible to Indians in a relatively unrestricted way for, unlike South Africa, there was nothing like *apartheid* after independence. While race may be less of a challenge for India, caste has been and continues to exert its influence, even if 'the vast majority of urban, educated, professional middle class in south India is now non-Brahmin' (Fuller and Narasimhan 2010: 494). For, at least in south India, Brahmins have as a caste managed to translate their 'presumptive success in [the] modern professions' (Fuller and Narasimhan 2010: 491), from their traditional claims to the modern one of presumptive intellectual superiority. These professions include law, medicine, engineering and information technology. In this, they are not dissimilar to certain traditional elites in Western society. Second, there are no policies to open up access to the professions as there is in South Africa. Most professionals would work as solo practitioners or as a member of a family practice (Ballakrishnen 2017: 327), at least up until 1991, when things began to change with the neo-liberal reforms of that year (Ballakrishnen 2016: 276, footnote 1). These reforms opened the professions to the global markets. This happened without any general or substantial increase in the number of women working within the professions, with one key exception. In general, women were employed in what would be seen traditionally as 'female-appropriate' professional roles, including Human Resource Management, communications work and in medicine, obstetrics and gynaecology (Ballakrishnen 2016: 271–272). It has not been because women were excluded from the professions but rather that the culture of the professions, and of wider society too, has been strongly patriarchal. It is this that consequently restricted the professional opportunities of women within India and this has remained the case even after the neo-liberal reforms. There has been, however, one very intriguing exception, which has emerged within the legal profession over recent decades. It relates to the new kinds of transactional work that have grown substantially in relation to international mergers and other globalised legal work (Ballakrishnen 2016: 267). This has given rise to new law firms to service this new work. These firms are protected by government regulations from direct influence of international firms reflecting a combination of protectionism and globalism. This, in turn, has led to an oasis of feminisation within law, as represented by this segment of the profession. To be successful, it seems, these new outwardly facing law firms have to demonstrate gender equality to reflect more the meritocratic cultures of international firms. There is, however, another reason, and that is in order to recruit the best graduates from the best law schools these firms need to reflect the gender equality embedded in the culture of those institutions too. Ballakrishnen (2016, 2017) provides an illustrative Indian case study, which brings out both the continuity and discontinuity with the historical experience reported by Dezalay and Garth (2010).

The legal profession within India continues along its path-dependent trajectory in maintaining an elite position within society along with a predominantly masculinist approach, but there are small signs that this male dominance may be beginning to erode in the face of globalisation. This contrasts with South Africa, where it is government policies that provide the main force working towards bringing about greater gender equality. These South African reforms are also intended to bring about greater racial equality, whereas in India the parallel inequality of caste, it has been argued, will evaporate over time with the growing opportunities for the expanding middle class of India (Fuller and Narasimhan 2010). How soon and how extensively caste will become an irrelevant anachronism within the professions, however, remains to be seen.

Intersectionality, social class and the professions

Intersectionality is not restricted to ethnicity and gender; social class also needs consideration. To take the example of Law, as one of the established professions, in the UK, the Law Society (2020: 28) reported that 63% of solicitors' parents were in occupations classified as professional, as compared to the general population where that figure is only 34%. If one takes attendance at an independent/private, fee-paying school as a measure of class advantage then the figures for Law, Medicine and the Military too are revealing as the Sutton Trust (2016) report shows: whereas 93% of the UK population attended state schools, 74% of the judiciary and 71% of barristers went to independent schools. Similarly, 71% of military officers and 61% of medical doctors. Interestingly, this is not the case for solicitors or journalists. To better explain this continuing class differences across the established professions research has taken a Bourdieusian turn. Recent research in this area has concentrated on cultural and social capitals. These are seen as providing a better understanding of recruitment and careers within the professions than simple 'snapshots' of class origins and destinations that characterised previous research (Laurison and Friedman 2016). Key to cultural capital, particularly in connection with professional careers, is that of education and credentials, which also tend to be transferred intergenerationally. This form of capital, however, can be further increased – or magnified – by the acquisition of an 'aesthetic disposition' (Bourdieu 1984) – for example, to art, music, foreign travel, architecture, fashion, cuisine and the list could go on longer. These signify social status, but not in any simple hierarchical sense, more of a mosaic or cluster of differing statuses that coalesce, for Bourdieu (1984) as *habitus*. The relevance to the professions is that their acquisition helps in gaining access into the professions (Laurison and Friedman 2016). In addition, it underpins a crucial aspect of their class position vis-à-vis their clients – and other professionals. In the USA Rivera and Tilcsik (2016: 1122) found that 'men who display markers of higher social classes are significantly more likely than other[s] . . . to be invited for interview for top law firm jobs'. In the UK Cook, Falconbridge and Muzio's (2012) study of 'London's legal elite', also based on a Bourdieusian analysis, came to similar conclusions as to the normalisation of upper-middle class cultural capital as the key into the profession. From their detailed analysis drawing on the UK Labour Force Study, Laurison and Friedman (2016) have been able to show the presence of a 'class ceiling', paralleling the gendered 'glass ceiling'. Professionals from working-class origins, once they have negotiated around these social and cultural capital obstacles, will then only earn an average of 83% as compared to their colleagues from middle-class origins, that is, those whose parents had higher managerial/professional jobs (Laurison and Friedman 2016: 679) which amounted to £7,350 ($11,000) per annum at the time of that research.

In the UK, Savage and colleagues have extensively researched social class based on cultural capital, including the implications for understanding the class and cultural differentiation for the professions (e.g. Le Roux, Rouanet, Savage and Warde 2008). Their later work includes direct consideration of the role of cultural and social capital in addition to economic capital for analysing social class Savage et al. 2013). Their model of social class set out in that article met with some hostile academic criticism. However, to discuss that debate here in any detail would take me too far away from the subject of professions and professionalism; nevertheless, one can get an overview of the debate from Savage et al.'s response in 'On social class, anno 2014' (Savage et al. 2015). The important point here is that the research of this group is methodologically sound and draws on a wide range of class analysis differences within and between professions. A good example of this is Laurison and Friedman's (2016) paper on the class pay gap in Britain's higher professional and managerial occupations. These authors present evidence of a 'class ceiling', as referred to earlier, in addition to the 'glass ceiling' long recognised as facing women and ethnic minorities (Davies 2011; Cohen and Huffman 2007). Another example is that of Giazitzoglu and Muzio's (2021) longitudinal study of the impact of the 'class ceiling' for working-class men within the IT profession, although this is described more in terms of the 'hidden injuries of class' (Sennett and Cobb 1972).

To find out the implications of race and/or gender intersectionality with social class and *vice versa* is very complex (Nash 2008; McCall 2005). Choroszewicz and Adams (2019) have approached this challenge by setting up an ideal professional as being middle-aged, middle class, dominant ethnicity and typically male (ibid.: 7) against which they identify and contrast *meta-work*, which is 'hidden, invisible work performed specifically by young, non-traditional and disadvantaged professionals' (ibid.: 7). This *meta-work*, however, is no *rite de passage* but an ongoing reality that reduces their career opportunities, a conclusion that underwrites much of the research cited earlier in this chapter.

Conclusion

This chapter described and reviewed the intrinsic inequalities historically embedded within the professions and examined the extent these may have been eradicated. The professions historically have been rooted in social exclusion and patriarchy and viewed as the vocation for the sons of the white upper-middle classes. By the latter end of the twentieth century this notion of the professions was being heavily criticised, most notably by feminist authors. By the first quarter of the twenty-first century, real progress on access to the professions has been made, to a greater or lesser extent. The patriarchal archetype has begun to give way to a newer model of a profession and professionalism, one that recruits and trains neophytes from across genders, races and ethnicities and classes. Yet, in this transformation, there remains clear evidence that the traditional patriarchal archetype is still haunting the professions, although possibly its presence will continue to fade. Although, if the influences of managerialism continue to hold sway, it is possible that meta-work – as Choroszewicz and Adams (2019) describe it – will become further institutionalised and continue to entrap many young women and men from different ethnicities, sexualities and working class in the more routine work of the professions.

References

All internet links accessed and checked on 24 May 2023 or later.

Abbott, A. (1988) *The System of Professions: an essay on the division of expert labor*. Chicago and London: The University of Chicago Press.

AICPA, see Association of International Certified Professional Accountants.

Association of International Certified Professional Accountants (AICPA) (2021) *2019 CPA Firm Gender Survey*. Available at https://us.aicpa.org/career/womeninthe profession.

Association of International Certified Professional Accountants (AICPA) (2019) *Trends in the supply of accounting graduates and the demand for public accounting recruits*.

Association of American Medical Colleges (AAMC) (2018) *Enrolment, Graduates, and MD-PhD Data*. Available at www.aamc.org/data/facts/enrollmentgraduate/

Acker, J. (2006) 'Inequality regimes: gender, class, and race in organisations'. *Gender & Society* 20(4): 441–464.

Ballakrishnen, S. (2016) 'India (International) Inc.: Global work and the (re)organization of professionalism in emerging economies'. In M. Dent, I. Bourgeault, J.-L. Denis and E. Kuhlmann (eds) *The Routledge Companion to the Professions and Professionalism*. London: Routledge: 265–279.

Ballakrishnen, S. (2017) '"She gets the job done": Entrenched gender meanings and new returns to essentialism in India's elite professional firms'. *Journal of Professions and Organizations*, 4: 324–342.

Bar Standards Board (2021) *Diversity at the Bar 2020*. London: Bar Standards Board. Available at www.barstandsboard.org.

Boiarintseva, G. and Richardson, J. (2019) 'Work-life balance and male lawyers: a socially constructed and dynamic process'. *Personnel Review*, 48(4): 866–879.

Bolton, S. and Muzio, D. (2008) 'The paradoxical processes of feminization in the professions: The case of established, aspiring and semi-professions'. *Work, Employment and Society*, 22 (2): 281–299.

Bonnin, D. and Rugganan, S. (2016) 'Professions and professionalism in emerging economies: The case of South Africa'. In M. Dent, I.L. Bourgeault, J.-L. Denis and E. Kuhlmann (eds) *The Routledge Companion to the Professions and Professionalism*. London: Routledge: 251–264.

Botezat, A. and Ramos, R. (2020) 'Physicians' brain drain–a gravity model of migration flows'. *Globalization and Health*, 16 (7). Available at https://doi.org/10.1186/s12992-019-0536-0

Bourdieu, P. (1984) *Distinction: a social critique of the judgement of taste*. London: Routledge & Kegan Paul.

Bourgeault, I.L., Wrede, S., Benoit, C. and Neiterman, E. (2016) 'Professions and the migration of expert labour: towards an intersectional analysis of transnational mobility patterns and integration pathways of health professionals'. In M. Dent,

I.L. Bourgeault, J.-L. Denis and E. Kuhlmann (eds) *The Routledge Companion to the Professions and Professionalism*. London: Routledge: 295–312.

Cech, E.A. (2022) LGBTQ@NASA at NASA and beyond: work structure and workplace inequality among LGBTQ STEM professionals. *Work and Occupations*, 49 (2): 187–228.

Cech, E.A. and Waidzunas, T.J. (2021) Systematic inequalities for LGBTQ professionals in STEM. *Science Advances, 7* (eabe0933): 1–9.

Choroszewicz, M. and Adams, T.L. (2019) 'Gender and age in the professions: Intersectionality, meta-work, and social change'. *Professions & Professionalism*, 9 (2): e3432.

Cohen, P.N. and Huffman, M.L. (2007) 'Working for the women? Female managers and the gender wage gap'. *American Sociology Review*, 72 (5): 681–704

Crompton, R. and Lynette, C. (2011) 'Women's career success and work-life adaptions in the accountancy and medical profession in Britain'. *Gender, Work and Organization*, 18 (2): 231–254.

Davies, C. (1996) 'The sociology of the professions and the profession of gender'. *Sociology*, 30 (4): 661–678.

Davies, Lord of Abersoch CBE (2011) *Women on Boards*. Department of Business, Innovation and Skills. Available at https://assets.publishing.service.gov.uk/government/uploads/system/uploads/attachment_data/file/31480/11-745-women-on-boards.pdf

Dent, M. (2002) 'Professional predicaments: Comparing the professionalisation projects of German and Italian nurses'. *International Journal of Public Sector Management*, 15 (2): 151–162.

Dent, M. (2003) *Remodelling Hospitals and Health Professions in Europe: Medicine, Nursing and the State*. Basingstoke: Palgrave.

Dent, M. (2008) 'Medicine, nursing and changing professional jurisdictions in the UK'. In D. Muzio, S. Ackroyd and J.-F. Chanlat (eds) *Redirections in the Study of Expert Labour*. Basingstoke: Palgrave Macmillan: 101–117.

Dent, M. (2017) 'Perspectives on professional identity'. In S.A. Webb (ed) *Professional Identity and Social Work*. London: Routledge: 21–34.

Dent, M. and Whitehead, S. (2002) 'Configuring the "new professional"'. In M. Dent and S. Whitehead (eds) *Managing Professional Identities: Knowledge, Performativity and the 'New' Professional*. London: Routledge: 1–16.

Dezalay, Y. and Garth, B.G. (2010) *Asian Legal Revivals*. Chicago and London: The University of Chicago Press.

Elliot, T., Earl, J. and Maher, T.V. (2017) 'Recruiting Inclusiveness: Intersectionality, Social Movements, and Youth Online'. *Non-State Violent Actors and Social Movement Organizations (Research in Social Movements, Conflicts and Change)*, 41: 279–311. Available at https://doi.org/10.1108/S0163-786X20170000041019

Esping-Andersen, G. (1990) *The Three Worlds of Welfare Capitalism*. Cambridge: Polity.

Etzioni, A. (ed) (1969) *The Semi-Professions and Their Organization: Teachers, Nurses, Social Workers*. London: Collier-Macmillan.

Eurostat (2018) *Statistics Explained: Healthcare Personnel Statistics – Physicians*. Available at https://ec.europa.eu/eurostat/statistics-explained/index.php/Healthcare_personnel_statistics_-_physicians

Evetts, J. (2011) 'A new professionalism? Challenges and opportunities'. *Current Sociology*, 59 (4): 406–422.

Faulconbridge, J.R. and Muzio, D. (2011) 'Professions in a globalizing world: towards a transnational sociology of the professions'. *International Sociology*, 27 (1): 136–152.

Financial Reporting Council (2021) *Key Facts and Trends in the Accountancy Profession*. London: The Financial Reporting Council Limited. Available at www.frc.org.uk/getattachment/669f6196-5a08-4a0b-aad3-b1915d4a6e4e/FRC-Key-Facts-Trends-2021.pdf

FNOPI (Federazione Nazionale Ordini Professioni Infermieristiche) (2021) *The Federation*. Available at www.Fnopi.it/en/the-federation.

Fuchs, C. (2018) Capitalism, patriarchy, slavery & racism in the age of digital capitalism & digital labour. *Critical Sociology*, 44 (4–5): 677–702.

Fuller, C.J. and Narasimhan, H. (2010) Traditional vocations and modern professions among Tamil Brahmans in colonial and post-colonial south India. *The Indian Economic and Social History Review*, 47 (4): 473–496.

General Medical Council (GMC) (2019) *The State of Medical Education and Practice in the UK: The workforce report*. London: GMC.

General Medical Council (GMC) (2020) *The State of Medical Education and Practice in the UK 2020*. General Medical Council. London. Available at https://www.gmc-uk.org/-/media/documents/somep-2020_pdf-84684244.pdf?la=en&hash=F68243A899E21859AB1D31866CC54A0119E60291.

Giazitzoglu, A. and Muzio, D. (2021) 'Learning the rules of the game: How is corporate masculinity learned and enacted by male professionals from nonprivileged backgrounds?' *Gender, Work & Organization*, 28: 67–84.

Hearn, J. (1982) 'Notes on patriarchy, professionalization and the semi-professions'. *Sociology*, 16 (2): 184–202.

Hearn, J. Biese, I., Choroszewicz, M. and Husu, L. (2016) 'Gender, diversity and intersectionality in professions and potential professions'. In M. Dent, I.L. Bourgeault, J-L Denis and E. Kuhlmann (eds) *The Routledge Companion to the Professions and Professionalism*. London: Routledge: 57–70.

Hearn, J. and Husu, L (2011) 'Understanding gender: Some implications for science and technology'. *Interdisciplinary Science Reviews*, 36: 103–113.

Hill, M. (2013) 'What is a welfare state?' In B. Greve (ed) *The Routledge Handbook of the Welfare State*. London: Routledge: 11–19.

Hilton, S.R. & Slotnick, H.B. (2005) 'Proto-professionalism: how professionalization occurs across the continuum of medical education'. *Medical Education*, 39: 58–65.

Kastoryano, R. (2010) 'Codes of otherness'. *Social Research*, 77 (1): 79–100.

Katz, F.E. (1969) 'Nurses'. In A. Etzioni (ed) *The Semi-Professions and Their Organization*. New York: The Free Press: 54–81.

Larson, M.S. (1977) *The Rise of Professionalism: A Sociological Analysis*. Berkeley, LA and London: University of California Press.

Laurison, D. and Friedman, S. (2016) 'The class pay gap in Britain's higher professional and managerial occupations'. *American Sociological Review*, 81 (4): 668–695.

Law Society (2020) *Diversity Profile of the Solicitors' Profession 2019*. The Law Society (Available at: www.lawsociety.org.uk).

Lorenzo, F.M.E., Galvez-Tan, J., Icamina, K. and Javier, L. (2007) 'Nurse migration form a source country perspective: Philippine country case study'. *Health Services Research*, 42 (3), Part II: 1406–1418, doi: 10.1111/j.1475-6773.2007.00716.x

Macdonald, K.M. (1995) *The Sociology of the Professions*. London: Sage.

McCall, L. (2005) 'The complexity of intersectionality'. *Signs*, 30: 1771–1800.

Milner, A., Baker, E., Jeraj, S. and Butt, J. (2020) 'Race-ethnic and gender differences in representation within the English NHS: A quantitative analysis'. *BMC Open*, 10: e034258, doi: 10.1136/bmjopen-2019-034258.

Misau, Y.A., Al-Sadat, N. and Gerei, A.B. (2010) 'Brain-drain and health care delivery in developing countries'. *Journal of Public Health Africa*, 1 (1): e6. http://doi:10.4081/jphia.2010.e6 PMID: 28299040; PMCID: PMC5345397

Nagel, J. (2003) *Race, Ethnicity and Sexuality: intimate intersections, forbidden frontiers.*

Nash, J.C. (2008) 'Re-thinking intersectionality'. *Feminist Review*, 89: 1–15.

National Association of Women Lawyers (2021) *2020 Survey Report: On the promotion and retention of women in law firms*. Available at https://issuu.com/nawl1899/docs/2021_nawl_survey_report/32 .

Neiterman, E. and Bourgeault, I.L. (2015) 'The shield of professional status: comparing internationally educated nurses' & international medical graduates' experience of discrimination'. *Health*, 19 (6): 615–634.

Pang, T., Langsang, M.A. and Haines, A. (2002) 'Brain drain and health professionals: A global problem needs global solutions'. *British Medical Journal (BMJ)*, 324 (7336): 499–500.

Patton, Jnr., A. (1996) *Physicians, Racism and Diaspora in West Africa*. Gainesville: University Press of Florida.

Porter, R. (2001b) *Quacks: Fakers and Charlatans in English Medicine*. Stroud: Tempus.

Rivera, L.A. and Tilcsik, A. (2016) 'Class advantage, commitment penalty: the gendered effect of social class signals in an elite labor market'. *American Sociological Review*, 81 (6): 1097–1131.

Savage, M., Devine, D., Cunningham, N., et al. (2015) 'On social class, anno 2014'. *Sociology*, 47 (2): 219–250.

Savage, M., Devine, D., Cunningham, N., et al. (2013) 'A new model of social class? Findings from the BBC's great British class survey experiment'. *Sociology*, 49 (6): 1011–1030.

Sennett, R. and Cobb, J. (1972) *The Hidden Injuries of Class*. Cambridge: Cambridge University Press.

Simmel, G. (1971) 'The Stranger' *Georg Simmel on Individuality and Social Forms*. Chicago: University of Chicago Press: 143–149.

Smith, D.M. and Gillin, N. (2021) 'Filipino nurse migration to the UK: Understanding migration choices from an ontological and security-seeking perspective'. *Social Science & Medicine*, 276: 113881, doi: 10.1016/j.socscimed.2021.113881.

Sommerlad, H. and Ashley, L. (2015) Diversity and Inclusion. In Empson, L, Muzio, D, Broschak, J. (Eds.) *The Oxford Handbook of Professional Service Firms*. Oxford: OUP: 452–475.

Stenger, S. and Roulet, T.J. (2018) 'Pride against prejudice? The stakes of concealment and disclosure of a stigmatized identity for gay and lesbian auditors'. *Work, Employment and Society*, 32 (2): 257–273.

van Schothorst-van Roekel, J., Weggelaar-Jansen, A.M.J.M.W., de Bont, A.A. and Wallenburg, I. (2020) 'The balancing act of organizing professionals and managers: An ethnographic account of nursing role development and unfolding nurse-manager relationships'. *Journal of Professions and Organization*, 7 (3): 283–299.

Westwood, S. (2022). 'Religious-based negative attitudes towards LGBTQ people among healthcare, social care and social work students and professionals: a review of the international literature'. *Health & Social Care in the Community*, 30, e1449–e1470.

Witz, A. (1992) *Professions and Patriarchy*. London: Routledge.

4 Governing and governance

Introduction

Governance is an intriguing term in relation to the professions, as traditionally professions have claimed, with some success, the right to govern themselves, yet governance implies being accountable to others. In general terms, it refers to the *process* of governing and it came into prominence in the 1980s (Bevir 2012: 16–18). The professions were caught up in its net early on, for governance has emerged as a central tenet in the relations between professions, the state and the public in the wake of New Public Management (NPM) (see also Chapter 5). In simple terms governance relates to social organisation and coordination (Bevir 2011: 23–25, 2012: 18); nevertheless, 'regulation' and 'control' are both often treated as similes for 'governance' even if there are marked differences in terms of emphasis and implications. Governance can be thought of as a 'soft bureaucracy', to borrow Courpasson's (2000) term, in contrast to the 'hard bureaucracy' many professionals experienced under New Public Management. Yet it is very different from the classic notion of professional autonomy, as previously enjoyed by lawyers and doctors.

Before going further, it is useful to consider the activity of governing, which resonates with governance (Burau 2016) even though it emphasises the role professions have in regulating others, rather than regulating themselves. This has been referred to as 'governmentality' drawing on Foucault's (1979) approach to the analysis of government, particularly within Western liberal democracies (Johnson 1995; Burau 2016: 93–94). This becomes most clear when government ministers justify their policy and practice by reference to the 'scientific evidence' provided by professional experts (Burau 2016). This is something that became really noticeable during the COVID crisis of 2020/2022 with medical and public health experts playing a key role in underpinning government policies. Governmentality, however, is not just apparent at times of crisis, for Foucault it constitutes an integral part of routine government. It means that the professions can enjoy high status and rewards because they are part of the governing apparatus – while also appearing to serve the interests of their clients. This ambiguity reflects the nature of organised

DOI: 10.4324/9780429430831-4

professions' general relationship with the state. In Foucauldian terms the professions are themselves part of the state (Johnson 1995; Evetts 2013: 6). Even if it is not uncommon for the ranks of a profession to contain radical groups among their membership (e.g. radical lawyers and doctors), or for an organised profession to criticise government policy, this does not undermine the argument. In Foucauldian terms what is most pertinent is that the complex interconnections that constitute governmentality – or 'government "at a distance"' (Fournier 1999: 182; Miller and Rose 2008: 32–35) – determines the ways in which professional autonomy, regulation and governance have been shaped.

For the purposes of this book one can reasonably suggest a periodisation that captures the (overlapping) shifts in the 'disciplinary logic' governing the professions from the era of the welfare state in the mid-twentieth century until now: (1) self-regulation and autonomy, (2) external regulation and managerialism and (3) governance, networks and 'soft bureaucracy'. These approximately reflect the now classic distinctions between 'networks', 'hierarchy' and 'markets' (e.g. Thompson, Frances, Levacic and Mitchell 1991) although each stage of 'disciplinary logic' is a hybrid admixture. This is especially so in the case of governance, networks and 'soft bureaucracy'. Adler and Kwon (2008: 140–141), for example, prefers to replace 'networks' with 'community' as they view networks as too general a term, and community emphasises the trust element within effective communities. In relation to the professions, key here would be collegiality. Freidson (2001: 59–60) also makes use of the classic triarchy in his well-known discussion of the occupational division of labour, identifying the 'free market', 'bureaucracy' and 'occupational' as alternative forms of control. Broadly, since the 1980s we see markets and (occupational/community) networks taking a more significant role in governance (Bevir 2012: 16, 2013). As with many typologies, while the three categories are analytically distinct, they reflect three intertwined organisational forms (Exworthy, Powell and Mohan 2010). In the neo-liberalism of current times the influence of the market has spread its influence across profession-state relations and even within the public sector. Although the degree to which this occurs varies across different countries (Tuohy 2012), for example, as Esping-Andersen's (1990) now-classic analysis of welfare state models shows, markets tend to predominate more in liberal Anglo-Saxon countries than, for example, in Nordic or Continental European countries (Esping-Andersen 1999:146; Dent 2003a). Hence, the blending of markets and hierarchy (bureaucracy), where it occurs, will tend to be weighted differently within the different welfare regimes. Note I am not referring here to professional 'hybrids' of 'mixed' occupational/organisational roles (see Chapter 5). Here the hybridisation relates to 'mixed' governance models – for example, bureaucracy mixed with entrepreneurialism (market) (Tuohy 2012). Nevertheless, there will be a connection to be made between the two insofar as hybrid professional roles reflect hybridised ('mixed') governance regimes.

The chapter will examine each of the governance and governmentality approaches in turn and in each case draw upon examples across the professions landscape, including both the public and private sectors.

1. Professional self-regulation and autonomy

To begin at the beginning, the professions have traditionally claimed their right to 'autonomy' and with it collegiality as the form of governance. This, in its modern form, became established in the nineteenth century with the rise of the liberal professions and became further embedded within the welfare state that emerged in the second half of the twentieth century. In the case of medical doctors (*physicians*), a key example, it has been their claim to 'clinical autonomy' that has been crucial. In sociological terms, this is, essentially, the *indetermination* component of what Jamous and Peloille (1970) identified as the *indetermination/determination (I/T)* ratio. It is defined by the profession by its very lack of definition, that is, the part of clinical work that 'escapes rules at a given historical moment' (Jamous and Peloille 1970: 112). It relates to that area of activity where the clinician (or other professional) applies their judgement in light of their experience and training, rather than following published rules as, for example, in the case of clinical guidelines (to be explained later). This concept can readily be applied to professionals more generally, although in varying degrees. Historically, *indetermination* would include guild 'mysteries' but today it has come to refer to those technical contingencies, task complexities and social relations associated with professional work (Freidson 1994: 86–89) that are not readily determined and controlled by formal managerial controls. This form of professional autonomy is the 'loosely coupled' (Weick 1976) or, in more institutionalist terms, 'de-coupled' (Meyer and Rowan 1991), activity of work organisations.

It was around the mid-twentieth century that the welfare state was established in its modern forms. This was particularly within Europe, Nordic countries and the Antipodes (Australia and New Zealand) as well as, in various forms, across North and South America (Greve 2013), while in Asia the impact has been less noticeable (Li 2013; Goodman and Peng 1996). The countries of the communist bloc of that period are not touched upon here, except to say that those countries of Eastern Europe that have since joined the European Community have to various degrees adopted a broadly continental model of the welfare state, although these post-communist countries welfare reforms have been somewhat disparagingly described as 'neo-liberalism by decay' (Saxonberg and Sirovátka 2009 quoted in Saxonberg 2013: 177). The welfare state, in its various forms, became and remained the dominant arrangement within Western capitalism until around the 1980s when its ascendancy was increasingly eroded by the forces of neo-liberalism (Miller and Rose 2008: 79–82). In addition to its broader impact (and benefits) for economies and societies, the welfare state substantially empowered the professions, particularly in the public sector. The post-war settlement in Europe and North America, in principle, involved state provision of health and educational services, education, housing and welfare support such that everyone was included. There has, however, been considerable variation in the ways these services have been provided (Greve 2013; Pollitt and Bouckaert 2017). In the process, the state became dependent upon the knowledge and expertise of many professions and were, broadly, content to trust these professions to regulate themselves. This was particularly true for not only the medical profession, but even the less autonomous, heteronomous professions (e.g. nursing, teaching and social work) were expected to be largely self-governing.

As for those professions working predominantly outside the public sector, such as law, accountancy and the emergent profession of management consultancy [Muzio, Aulakh and Kirkpatrick 2019; Muzio and Kirkpatrick 2011), they did not come under scrutiny until the rise of neo-liberalism at the end of the twentieth century. Sociologically, the period before NPM favoured neo-Weberian analyses premised as it is on 'social closure' (Saks 2017; Macdonald 1995; Witz 1992) and even if some profession's 'jurisdictions' were less influential than others (e.g. Nursing compared to Medicine) the work situation was collectively regulated more by the organised profession than by management. The era of the welfare state started to erode from the 1980s onwards as neo-liberalism established its dominance and NPM provide new ways of organising professional work within the public sector.

2. External regulation and managerialism

With the rise of neo-liberalism, which was particularly associated with the Reagan administration of the USA in the 1980s, it was emulated by the Conservative administration of Margaret Thatcher in the UK (as well as more notoriously by Pinochet's military dictatorship in Chile). The impact of this economic philosophy continues to be felt today, although less keenly than in previous decades. It remains very much a touchstone for libertarian conservatives. In terms of its impact on the organised professions, it is useful to examine neo-liberalism's developments in the UK, particularly in the guise of New Public Management (NPM). NPM became the model that informed neo-liberal developments across Europe, including the Nordic countries (Dent 2003a). The policy was concerned with de-regulation and a reduced role for an otherwise 'overloaded' state (e.g. Pierre 2000: 4), or so the argument ran. Somewhat counter-intuitively, it led to the professions experiencing higher levels of regulations, both institutionally and in their day-to-day work. The premise for this development was the state's growing distrust of the professions' own ability to self-govern themselves at least in line with the neo-liberal thinking of the time. For the policy thinkers the distrust was rooted in the 'theory of the firm' (Coase 1937) in which firms – and by extension, it can be argued, work organisations more generally – limit the functioning of the free market. But this can be overcome, or at least minimised, by viewing the organisational actors as being in contractual relationships to ensure proper compliance (Ouchi 1991: 246–247; Williamson 2002).

The organised professions were not convinced by neo-liberal ideas, especially when the result looked like a serious encroachment on their professional autonomy. Consequently, in the UK, the move to the new system of governance initially came about through direct government attacks to intended to de-legitimise the professions (Muzio and Ackroyd 2008: 35). These were somewhat helped, in the 1990s, by several instances of very serious professional misconduct. Within the UK medical profession there was a series of medical scandals, notably the cases of paediatric cardiac surgery at Bristol Royal Infirmary and, even worse, that of Harold Shipman GP. Both involved the unnecessary deaths of patients (Salter 2004; Klein 2001). There was also the furore around the retention of patients' organs at Alder Hey Hospital, Liverpool, at around the same time, which raised serious questions around informed consent (Salter 2004: 56). All of this, and the public enquiries associated with them, left that profession in a much-weakened position in its relations with government. There were similar revelations relating to other professions including Accountancy, as in the Enron case (Maltby 2008: 391). These scandals seriously undermined the organised professions' case for self-governance and opened the way for the implementation of new systems of management and scrutiny (governance).

The major managerial impact was felt most within the public sector, and there were two main thrusts to the policies; first, marketisation – and commodification of public services. 'Professional expertise [is being] . . . viewed as . . . an esoteric commodity . . . to be purchased on . . . [a] contractual basis' is how Muzio, Ackroyd and Chanlat (2008: 25) have described the development. Second, managerial oversight if not control of professional work. The result became known as New Public Management (NPM) (Dent and Barry 2004) largely because of the influential set of papers produced by Christopher Hood at the time (1991, 1995). This new regime that had started with a 'market' agenda increasingly shifted – or 'hybridised' – into a more 'managerialist' one and with it an even greater emphasis on performance measures and targets. Within the professions' governance discourse hybridisation refers to the 'blending' or 'co-existence' of two or more systems of social coordination and organisation of professional work, for example, hierarchy and market, as in the case of delivering public sector services (e.g. health, education) through private sector organisations, all within a context of professional (network) governance (Tuohy 2012). In many respects, all governance arrangements for professionals are hybrid, it simply depends on the relative weight given to particular elements of the triarchy (hierarchy, market or network) of systems of coordination and control. Thus, professional self-regulation is theoretically about network governance, but pragmatically, particularly within the public sector, it will also co-exist with a degree of hierarchical (or bureaucratic) coordination. Even private sector professionals, for example, in law and accountancy, will find their systems of self-governance subject to market influences and, even more noticeably, hierarchical ones within the world of corporate professional firms (Brock, Powell and Hinings 1999; Muzio and Kirkpatrick 2011).

The shift within the public sector to NPM reflected the state's attempt to wrest control from the professionals who were, in effect, had been running the public sector. While the strategy achieved considerable managerial change, the realities and complexities of professional work have meant that it could only be effective if it positively engaged with the professionals. It is a sad truism that while professionals do not always live up to their sworn high ethical standards, management has never been trusted by the public as much as their professional colleagues (Brown and Flores 2018: 52; Halliwell 2008: 428; Calnan and Sandford 2004). More generally, in the minds of many, the core values of public service of equity and social justice were undermined by the priority given to efficiency and 'value for money' (Ferlie 2012: 240). With the greater emphasis on markets – or quasi-markets – and networks there was a fragmentation of services, which weakened the centre's ability to steer and raised real concerns around public accountability. This led to what might be referred to as post-NPM reforms that coalesced into a New Public Governance (NPG) narrative (Newman 2001; Osborne 2006, 2010; Ferlie 2012). Similarly, and along a similar timeline, in the private sector, there emerged the New Governance Regulations (NGR) (Aulakh and Kirkpatrick 2018: 167), which will also be discussed in the next section.

3. Governance, networks and 'soft bureaucracy'

There are at least two strands to New Public Governance (NPG); one that emphasises networks and systems integration (Ferlie 2012: 240), and the other assumes that the professional networks are located within larger governance structures and the whole ambivalently structured and held together 'through sophisticated management strategies' (Courpasson 2000: 142). The first strand is associated with *networks* (Rhodes 1996; Osborne 2006, 2010; Bevir 2011, 2012) held together by shared values and norms (Bevir 2013: 59) underpinning interdependence and trust. The second, which has been called '*soft bureaucracy*' (Courpasson 2000), is based on the notion of loosely coupled organisations that corresponds to Meyer and Rowan's (1991) description of formal organisations as being necessarily de-coupled but this being disguised by 'myth and ceremony'. In essence 'soft bureaucracy' means allowing – or accepting – a group to self-govern itself so long as they do not breach over-arching organisation regulations. Ferlie's (2012: 240) NPG argument is not so very different, for NPG 'is less concerned with increasing levels of efficiency and productivity' as in the case under NPM, but in 'rebuild[ing] systemic capacity across a fragmented service delivery system' (2012: 240) (for 'fragmented' one might read 'loosely- or de-coupled'). There is an emphasis on 'quality-led approaches to service redesign' (ibid.: 240), which focus on the logic of quality improvement that formally connects the professions to their clients/patients/users within a user involvement discourse (Dent and Pahor 2015). This in turn makes the professional accountable not only to their peers, and their clients, but also implicitly to managerial influence, if not control. However, under NPG the professions have largely accommodated to the new reality and have accepted the need for their own direct involvement with management work, at least in some hybrid form (see Chapter 5). From a governmentality perspective NPG reflects 'action at a distance' (Miller and Rose 2008: 33–34). In consequence, professionals as 'free actors' find themselves subject to a new discourse that incorporates the quality improvement and user involvement as part of their own their own self-governance. Here it would be useful to provide some concrete examples of NPG. First, medicine and nursing, because of the ambivalent synergy between the two in their relations with each other and governments. Then, law and social work, which do not appear to have the same kind of synergy between them.

Medicine and nursing

The main strands of NPG that have infiltrated the work of doctors and nurses are related to clinical governance, a process that started with medical audit (Dent 2018: 19) which was introduced in the wake of the medical scandals discussed earlier, evolved into clinical audit and then changed from a retrospective to a prospective system with the introduction of clinical guidelines and care pathways (Dent and Tutt 2014: 177–178; Allen 2009) Now 'mistakes', in principle, are no longer simply detected and discussed (as in audit meeting), but factored out of the process, so long as everyone follows the guidelines and pathways (and these fit the circumstances – which they cannot all the time, because clinical cases can be complex). The path to the current models of guidelines began with medical audit (Dent 2018: 19, 2008: 106–108) but transmuted into clinical audit which relied on nursing rather than doctors (who had proven sluggish in embracing the new modes of governance (Dent 2008: 108–110). It is not that nursing particularly welcomed the new managerialism, but it had its mitigations not least with its role with clinical audit, guidelines and care pathways for it provided nursing with a new and growing professional jurisdiction (Dent and Tutt 2014; Allen 2009). Along this path of quality improvement, the patient has become, at least formally, both a co-producer and the rationale for the system of governance (Dent 2018; Dent and Pahor 2015). This has reconfigured the countervailing powers between not only state and medical profession (Light 1995) but between all the actors within the health care network (Dent 2006; Dent 2003a, 2003b; Burrage, Jarausch and Siegrist 1990). The potential for complexity here is greater than it might first appear. For example, medicine and management (and patients) within one organisation (e.g. a hospital) may be allies, or not, in face of broader threats to their organisation and its services (Dent 2003b). Similarly, the patient as user/consumer may not be an individual but either a combination of patients and carers or, simply, a cipher to justify a policy (usually based on patient surveys). Then there is the 'public' as encapsulated in 'Public Patient Involvement' (Dent and Pahor 2015) directly involved in policy decisions around the provision of services. But the public as citizens do have a governance role, particularly within deliberative forums, which, within the UK are now found across the health community (e.g. Hospital User Groups, Clinical Commissioning Groups) (Dent and Pahor 2015). Changes in the management of hospitals and clinics have also been significant; this was a move from an administrative to a managerialist role, with the implementation of NPM. Nevertheless, management *qua* management needed nurses and doctors to be involved in management decision-making to ensure credibility and legitimacy (Kirkpatrick 2016; Kirkpatrick, Jespersen, Dent and Neogy 2009). The policy's intent was to incorporate the professions within the new managerialism, but it is also the case that some medics, and nurses (Dent 2008), have seen involvement with management as a useful and necessary means of ensuring the profession maintains an influence within their organisations (Dent and Barry 2004; Kirkpatrick, Jespersen, Dent and Neogy 2009). These changes have been significant in terms of governmentality, as well as that of management and leadership to be discussed in the next chapter. The jurisdictions of medicine and nursing have their own ambivalent configuration (Dent 2008) usefully illustrated by the fact that in those countries where there are fewer doctors relative to population the nursing profession enjoys higher status and specialisation (Dent 2003a: 23), as in the Anglo-American world, than elsewhere. By contrast, where there are more doctors trained than the medical labour market can support the status, rewards and opportunities for nurses are much poorer. This has tended to be the case in Southern Mediterranean countries. However, in general terms, this is not the case with other possible professional pairings, for example, lawyers and social workers, where there is little overlap in jurisdictions.

Law and social work

There has long been a distinction made between occupational and organisational professions and professionals (Evetts 2013), or 'collegiate' and 'corporate' in the words of Muzio and Kirkpatrick (2011), touching on the realities of law, accountancy and similar professional services work today. Whereas medicine and nurses are professions that typically share a common space (clinics) this is much less so in the case of law and social work. Nevertheless, they provide a useful comparison in this review of professional governance, given they occupy similar positions in the division of expert labour to medicine and nursing, that is, one has claims to being a collegiate, liberal profession (law), the other an organisational profession predominantly in state employment and subject to centralised regulations, a product (in its modern form) of the welfare state (Rogowski 2010). Social work shares a similar pedigree to nursing and teaching. The profession of social work, however, unlike nursing, does include a significant radical strand that would happily dismiss its professional status on the grounds that it is elitist and not in the interests of the clients/service users (Pease 2013: 33). At the same time social workers remain concerned and critical that other professions do not take their work seriously enough. This particularly relates to the medical profession, whose members are – we are told – given to rejecting the 'diagnostic or therapeutic contribution of social workers' (Adams, Dominelli and Payne 2009: 171). This is a symptom that reflects the continuing 'Berlin Wall' between social and health care (Adams, Dominelli and Payne 2009: 169).

The legal profession, by contrast, enjoys its high status and autonomy. Traditionally the organisational model is the professional partnership, the P2 type identified by Greenwood, Hinings and Brown (1990) and which has become increasingly counterpoised to the Managerial Professional Business (MPB) archetype, characterised by managerialism and business values, even if retaining elements of the P2 emphasis on professionalism and partnership (Powell, Brock and Hinings 1999). The MPB has become the archetype for the global corporate professional services firms (PSFs) industry. These professional organisations have more in common with multi-national corporations than collegiate partnerships. In the UK they employ over 25% of all solicitors (Kirkpatrick and Noordegraaf 2015).

Governance for lawyers has in recent decades moved from an audit-based regulation model to one based more on self-governance. This latter approach is not the same as traditional collegiality insofar as the rules being followed are set centrally and there are clear mandated procedures and practices to be followed (Flood 2011; Aulakh and Kirkpatrick 2018). This new form of 'self-governance' has been labelled 'new governance' regulation (NGR) (Aulakh and Kirkpatrick 2018: 167) and has much in common with New Public Governance (NPG) discussed earlier. It marks a shift from 'rule-based' to a 'risk-based' system of governance (see also Lloyd-Bostock and Hunter 2008). This general movement gained momentum across corporate as well as professional organisations because of the greater adaptability, flexibility and cost-effectiveness that a risk-based approach would appear to offer (Ford 2008). In the case of the legal profession (and other professional services, including audit and accountancy) the new regulatory framework also marked a general move from individual to entity accountability based on an outcomes framework (Aulakh and Kirkpatrick 2018). In short, the law firms are now responsible for governance, subject to their procedures being judged 'fit for purpose' by the relevant overarching regulatory agency. There is one characteristic of law firms – and professional services in general – that raises concerns around these new governance arrangements. The firms are often globalised professional services firms (GPSF) (Flood 2011) with an international reach that extends way beyond the jurisdictions of national authorities. Other 'big players' at the transnational level include the EU (European Union) and GATS (General Agreement on Trade in Services) (Flood 2011) along with the indirect but possibly significant influence of 'sophisticated, knowledgeable, corporate clients' (Flood 2011: 513). The latter can at times have a far-from-benign effect on professional practice, as in the celebrated Enron scandal (Muzio, Aulakh and Kirkpatrick 2019: 36, Box 3.3) that led to the collapse of Arthur Andersen, the legal arm of Andersen Worldwide (Flood 2011: 508). This disaster played a significant role in the argument for the move away from the prior 'rule-based' approach to the current 'risk-based' one. In the process, the form the new governance arrangements took (a consequence of the lobbying by the GPSFs [Flood 2011]) has meant the larger global firms have been able to manage their own governance arrangements with relatively little involvement of national regulators (Flood 2011; Faulconbridge and Muzio 2011). The newer 'entity' governance arrangements reflect the corporatisation of the profession's services, which has already led to a stratification within the profession; the status differentials between the partners and salaried lawyers coupled with the increased specialisation, especially within these larger organisations. NGR has permeated across the whole range of law firms, in Aulakh and Kirkpatrick's (2018) study of solicitor practices in England and Wales, for example, there appeared to be no major differences between the large corporate firms and smaller regional practices. However, one issue of concern is the finding that the NGR was undermining the enculturation of lawyers in the values and ethics of professionalism, especially within the large corporate law firms (Aulakh and Kirkpatrick 2018: 176–178). The reason appears to be the centralisation in the role of the compliance officers of the oversight of these professional matters (values and ethics). These have also been systematised within computer-based legal-practice case management systems, which have the added facility for managers to monitor professional work and professional staff productivity (Aulakh and Kirkpatrick 2018: 175).

This is a good place to switch the focus back to the social workers, for their work too is organised in terms of case management underpinned by protocolised pathways (Payne 2000). Although here the professionals' responses are rather different for Social Work represents a different kind of profession to that of law, one more in line with nursing and teaching. It developed in its modern form with the growth of the welfare state in the twentieth century (Evetts 2013). Within Social Work in the UK, it is probably Rogowski's (2010) book *Social Work: The rise and fall of a profession?* that captures the anger and frustration that many in the profession have felt. Unlike nursing, the impact of NPM on social work has been experienced as almost wholly negative. Social workers found themselves transformed from being front-line professionals to being contractors of services from the third and private sectors, which reflected the shift to marketisation. By the turn of the millennium, however, just as elsewhere, there was a discernible shift to governance (Frahm and Martin 2009; Carson, Chung and Evans 2015). Frahm and Martin's (2009: 409) argument is that *hierarchy* and *networks* and *marketisation* within social work are in opposition to each other, which they call 'duelling paradigms'. Here *markets* are the antithesis to *government* (i.e. *hierarchy*), which lead to *governance*, but equally, *government* (*hierarchy*) and *governance* (networks) are in opposition too, as 'thesis' and 'antithesis'. They suggest that there were other duelling paradigms active in the 1980s and 1990s including NPM (Frahm and Martin 2009: 408) but these were secondary to the *government* and *markets* paradigms. It is from the contradictions between the two logics (*government* [or *hierarchy*] and *market*) that a new paradigm (or archetype) emerged, viz. *governance*. While this looks to be of a *network* type it also contains elements of the other archetypes; *hierarchy (government)* and *markets*. It is important to note that Frahm and Martin (2009) do not use or reference the notion of archetypes (cf. Greenwood and Hinings 1993) but use the term 'paradigm'. However, by introducing this alternative, the model becomes more accessible to an organisational and institutional analysis (Powell and DiMaggio 1991). The analysis forefronts what has been the central experience for social workers, namely the challenge of marketisation. In consequence, the *governance* synthesis is understood as an elaboration of a system intended to further undermine social workers' discretion (autonomy) and professional status. This brings us to another archetype, relevant to the issue of governance, that has become integral to any understanding of social, the 'street level bureaucrats' (Lipsky 1980, 2010), who can be described as:

> [p]ublic service workers who interact directly with citizens in the course of their jobs, and who have substantial discretion in the execution of their work.
> (Lipsky 1980: 3)

Street-level bureaucracies generally cover a wide range of occupations and professions including teachers, police officers and health workers. It has, however, taken a particularly deep root within social work. The social, financial and political complexity of social work and its dynamics is such that the front-line social worker has had of necessity to exercise a degree of discretion and judgement. This, on the face of it, places their status clearly within the professional domain, on a par with medics in terms of clinical autonomy – except that the street-level bureaucrat has at times been assumed to exercise their discretion for their own benefit (Carson, Chung and Evans 2015: 173). This also has much in common with the notion of 'loose coupling' (Weick 1976) or 'de-coupling' (Meyer and Rowan 1991), which means that there is uncertainty about how work is to be carried out in the best interest of the client. In the broader picture, however, this is rarely clear cut, as when policy is complex and/or ill-defined. For example, in dealing *fully* with one client other clients may be denied support, because of a lack of resources. Governance, ideally, has to be able to tolerate the loose-coupled or de-coupled varieties of workplace discretion, but acute enough to identify any illicit 'uncoupling' and trigger appropriate action to deal with it.

Having provided some context, the attention turns now and in more detail onto the specific examples of governance, namely protocols and pathways.

Protocols and pathways

Social work operates within a very different work situation to that of nursing, where protocolised rule following is well established and accepted. Within social work this has not been the case. Social workers and their clients have had some experience of care pathways (Webb 2006; Payne 2000), for example, early intervention to avoid child/infant abuse (Barlow, Dawe, Coe and Harnett 2016), or supporting elderly individuals move between hospital, home or care home (e.g. Nakashima, Chapin, Macmillan and Zimmerman 2005). However, the model introduced is a highly structured one ostensibly based on evidence-based practice equivalent to the clinical guidelines and care pathways used within health care (Webb 2002). A key example illustrating the difference with health care is the challenges of proceduralisation (or standardisation) that came with the introduction of computer-based assessment forms linked to the *Looking after Children* (LAC) system introduced in UK social work departments in the 1990s (Garrett 2004: 55). This was followed up with the *Framework for the Assessment of Children in Need and their Families* (Garrett 2004: 55; Department of Health 2000). The LAC's most tangible legacy for social workers is the forms designed to capture the data and information deemed necessary for the management of each case. Rogowski (2010: 92) criticises – with irony – the approach for being less interested in the client than:

> First, ensuring that young people are adequately prepared for the 'world of work' and that they are compliant, well-presented employees who can function in 'flexible' markets; and second, focusing on the need to ensure that the 'crimo-genic' proclivities of children of the unemployed and poor are detected, regulated and controlled.

Also, more broadly, for being:

> Uncritical [in its] acceptance of current economic and social arrangements . . . [and] presented as the unquestioned foundations of familial dynamics and interpersonal relationships.
>
> (Rogowski 2010: 93–94)

The associated fragmentation of social work 'amounts to deskilling' (Rogowski 2010: 92) and 'deprofessionalisation' (Rogowski 2010: 107). Garrett (2004), also a critic of proceduralisation, views development as particularly problematic. Partly because the documentation – the assessment schedules – can be alienating for the clients, because the social worker seems more interested in completing the electronic forms than relating directly with them and their concerns (Garrett 2004) and undermining any effective 'pastoral care' (Martin and Waring 2018). Much of this has also been reflected in professional concerns with the development of similar systems within health care (Dent 1996) although these have subsequently become normalised (Dent and Tutt 2014). For social workers, it would appear that this has not happened to the same extent. In large part, unlike the nurses (Allen 2014), this is because they do not feel in control of the process. Moreover, it is experienced as putting distance between themselves and their clients. This distancing, for social workers, has been further extended with the shift to contracting and outsourcing a direct result of NPM.

From the opening decade of the millennium, NPM gave way to more complex networked relationships and alliances across government agencies and the third sector (Carson, Chung and Evans 2015: 171). A process leading to a form of New Public Governance (NPG):

> Neither the market contractualism of NPM nor the social contractualism and network governance of post-neoliberal collaborations [i.e. NPG] have resolved the variation[s in the field], which derives from worker discretion and the ensuing policy and service delivery implementation gaps. Contractualism within the arena of social policy does not give managers increased control over front-line staff but, rather, adds *more layers and interstices, where multiple points of discretion need to be documented and understood.*
>
> (Carson, Chung and Evans 2015, 2015: 181 *emphases added*)

This moves us beyond the adversarial character of Lipsky's (1980) classic dichotomy between bureaucracy and practice, but in ways more to do with building and sustaining good contracting relationships and networks than in direct client relations:

> [T]here will always be variation in front-line practice, it cannot be attributed simply to the discretion of practitioners, but rather it reflects the range of intricate transactions between policy developments and front-line practice.
>
> (Carson, Chung and Evans 2015: 180)

All of this highlights the dilemma for these professionals, in enjoying their formal professional status and protected labour market shelter (Freidson 2001), it is expected that their work contributed to the good government of society. In Foucault's terms, professional work is an integral part of governmentality (Martin and Waring 2018; Johnson 1995). This has not precluded professionals being critical of this reality, and this is very clear in the case of social work with its 'foundational values of equality and justice' (Gray and Webb 2013: 3) leading to a number within the profession taking a political stand to defend those values (ibid.: 3). As a consequence, there is a view within the profession that questions whether they should even be a profession, because that is elitist and concerned more with their own interests than those of their clients (Rogowski 2010: 109). Even so, it is an organised profession, which in the UK has – since 2019 – come under the umbrella of Professional Standards Authority for Healthcare and Social Care (PSA) (Worsley, Beddoe, McLaughlin and Teater 2020). This is the body that since 2002 'regulates the regulators', which are the appointed professional councils (Allsop and Jones 2018: 93). Within health care it is called clinical governance, which is the system of oversight that is part of the broader 'performativity' culture in the health care sector, one that has been reflected across other professionals within the public sector (e.g. education, social work) as well as professions working outside the public sector too (e.g. law and accounting). This has commonly manifested itself – as Muzio, Aulakh and Kirkpatrick (2019: 41–42) explain – as an external audit for monitoring professional's work (Verbeeten and Speklé 2015). This led to league tables not only of hospitals but also of schools and other public sector organisations. This form of performance management 'measured' schools, hospitals as well as social work departments against pre-set performance indicators. This was sometimes referred to as 'targets and terror' but also led to a 'gaming' the system (Bevan and Wilson 2013) typically by 'hitting the target and missing the point' (Bevan and Hood 2006: 521). To combat gaming semi-independent agencies were set up to audit public sector organisations. In England these include the Office for Standards in Education, Children's Services and Skills (OFSTED) for schools and the Care Quality Commission (CQC) for health and social care. This approach to professional governance also gave the management a *raison d'etre* within these organisations for they have taken on the function of monitoring and steering their organisation's professionals' performance typically on their 'dashboards'. The continued existence of the regulatory bodies shows that NPG is not only a system of self- cum networked- governance (Rhodes 1996) but clearly exhibits elements of 'soft bureaucracy' (Courpasson 2000). The regulatory authorities provide 'a rigid exterior appearance symbolising what key stakeholders expect but with a loosely coupled set of interior practices' (e.g. Sheaff et al. 2003: 409) which requires – as well as providing – the space for the exercise of professional work autonomy or discretion. Although that does not change the fact that professional organisations are now subject to greater scrutiny than ever before.

Conclusion

Governance for the professions has evolved and in its current complex form is an admixture of hierarchy, markets and networks, with one element usually being dominant at any time. However, with the neo-liberal turn in the latter decades of the twentieth century the 'market' became an ever-present reality in professional governance, as elsewhere. This has been particularly obvious within the workings of NPM. But, despite it being ubiquitous 'marketisation' has not been the only, or necessarily, the dominant force. The general shift of emphasis has been from managerialist NPM to NPG and with that a change in emphasis from performance targets to protocols and guidelines, that is, from *retrospective* to *prospective* quality controls. These processes have changed the work situation of the professions and what it means to be a professional. The new systems of governance put a much greater emphasis on teamwork and away from the individual practitioner, it has also brought about a greater involvement of management (in overseeing the professionals' organisational performance including measures of their quality of work). It is to this subject of managerialism as it impacts and involves professionals that we now turn to.

References

All internet links accessed and checked on 24 May 2023 or later.

Adams, R., Dominelli, L. and Payne, M. (2009) *Practicing Social Work in a Complex World*. Basingstoke: Palgrave Mcmillan.

Adler, P.S., and Kwon, S.-W. (2008) 'Community, market and hierarchy in the evolving organization of professional work: The case of medicine'. In D. Muzio, S. Ackroyd and J.-F. Chanlat (eds) *Redirections in the Study of Expert Labour: Established Professions and New Expert Occupations*. Basingstoke: Palgrave Macmillan: 139–160.

Allen, D. (2009) 'From boundary concept to boundary object: The practice and politics of care pathway development'. *Social Science & Medicine*, 69: 354–361.

Allen, D. (2014) 'Lost in translation? "Evidence" and the articulation of institutional logics in integrated care pathways: From positive to negative boundary object?' *Sociology of Health and Illness*, 36 (6): 807–822.

Allsop, J. and Jones, K. (2018) 'Regulating the regulators: The rise of the United Kingdom professional standards authority'. In J.M. Chamberlain, M. Dent and M. Saks (eds) *Professional Health Regulation in Public Interest: International Perspectives*. Bristol: Policy Press: 93–116.

Aulakh, S. and Kirkpatrick, I. (2018) 'New governance regulation and lawyers: When substantive compliance erodes legal professionalism'. *Journal of Professions and Organizations*, 5: 167–183.

Barlow, J., Dawe, S., Coe, C. and Harnett, P. (2016) 'An evidence-based, pre-birth assessment pathway for vulnerable pregnant women'. *British Journal of Social Work*, 46: 960–973.

Bevan, G. and Hood, C. (2006) 'What's measured is what matters: Targets and gaming in the English public health care system'. *Public Administration*, 84 (3): 517–538.

Bevan, G. and Wilson, D. (2013) 'Does "naming and shaming" work for schools and hospitals? Lessons from natural experiments in England and Wales'. *Public Money & Management*, 33 (4): 245–252.

Bevir, M. (2011) 'Governance as theory, practice and dilemma'. In M. Bevir (ed) *The Sage Book of Governance*. London: Sage: 21–44.

Bevir, M. (2012) *Governance: A Very Short Introduction*. Oxford: Oxford University Press.
Bevir, M. (2013) *A Theory of Governance*. Berkeley, LA and London: University of California Press. Available at https://escholarship.org/uc/item/2qs2w3rb
Brock, D.M., Powell, M.J., and Hinings, C.R. (1999) 'The restructured professional organization: Corporates, cobwebs and cowboys'. In D. Brock, M. Powell and C.R. Hinings (eds) *Restructuring the Professional Organization: Accounting, Health Care and Law*. London: Routledge: 215–229.
Brown, P. and Flores, R. (2018) 'The informalization of professional-patient interactions and the consequences for regulation in the United Kingdom'. In M. Dent, I.L. Bourgeault, J.-L. Denis and E. Kuhlmann (eds) *The Routledge Companion to the Professions and Professionalism*. London: Routledge: 39–59.
Burau, V. (2016) 'Governing through experts'. In M. Dent, I.L. Bourgeault, J.-L. Denis and E. Kuhlmann (eds) *The Routledge Companion to the Professions and Professionalism*. London: Routledge: 91–101.
Burrage, M., Jarausch, K. and Siegrist, H. (1990) 'An actor-based framework for the study of the professions'. In M. Burrage and R. Torstendahl (eds) *Professions in Theory and History*. London: Sage: 203–225.
Calnan, M. and Sandford, E. (2004) 'Public trust in healthcare: The system or the doctors?'. *Quality & Safety in Healthcare*, 13: 92–97.
Carson, E., Chung, D. and Evans, T. (2015) 'Complexities of discretion in social services in the third sector'. *European Journal of Social Work*, 18 (2): 167–184.
Coase, R. (1937) 'The nature of the firm'. *Economica*, 4: 386–405.
Courpasson, D. (2000) 'Managerial strategies of domination, power in soft bureaucracies'. *Organization Studies*, 21 (1): 141–161.
Dent, M. (1996) *Professions, Information Technology and Management in Hospitals*. Aldershot: Avebury.
Dent, M. (2003a) *Remodelling Hospitals and Health Professions in Europe: Medicine, Nursing and the State*. Basingstoke: Palgrave.
Dent, M. (2003b) 'Managing doctors and saving a hospital: Irony, rhetoric and actor networks'. *Organization*, 10 (1): 107–127.
Dent, M. (2006) 'Disciplining the medical profession? Implications of patient choice for medical dominance'. *Health Sociology Review*, 15 (5): 458–468.
Dent, M. (2008) 'Medicine, nursing and changing professional jurisdictions in the UK'. In D. Muzio, S. Ackroyd and J.-F. Chanlat (eds) *Redirections in the Study of Expert Labour*. Basingstoke: Palgrave Macmillan: 101–117.
Dent, M. (2018) 'Health care governance, user involvement and medical regulation in Europe'. In J.M. Chamberlain, M. Dent and M. Saks (eds) *Professional Health Regulation in the Public Interest: International perspectives*. Bristol: Policy Press: 17–37.
Dent, M. and Barry, J. (2004) 'New public management and the professions in the UK: Reconfiguring control?'. In M. Dent, J. Chandler and J. Barry (eds) *Questioning the New Public Management*. Aldershot: Ashgate: 7–20.
Dent, M. and Pahor, J. (2015) 'Patient involvement in Europe–a comparative framework'. *Journal of Health Organization and Management*, 29 (5): 546–555.
Dent, M. and Tutt, D. (2014) 'Electronic patient information systems and care pathways: The organisational challenges of implementation and integration'. *Health Informatics Journal*, 20 (3): 176–188.
Department of Health (2000) *Assessing Children in Need and their Families: Practice Guidance*. London: Stationary Office.

Esping-Andersen, G. (1990) *The Three Worlds of Welfare Capitalism*. Cambridge: Polity.

Esping-Andersen, G. (1999) *Social Foundations of Post-industrial Economics*. Cambridge: Polity Press.

Evetts, J. (2013) 'Professionalism: Values and ideology'. *Current Sociology*, 61 (5–6): 778–796.

Exworthy, M., Powell, M. and Mohan, J. (2010) 'Markets, bureaucracy and public management: The NHS: Quasi-market, quasi-hierarchy and quasi-network?'. *Public Money & Management*, 19 (4): 15–22.

Faulconbridge, J.R. and Muzio, D. (2011) 'Professions in a globalizing world: Towards a transnational sociology of the professions'. *International Sociology*, 27 (1): 136–152.

Ferlie, E. (2012) 'Concluding discussion: Paradigms and instruments of public management reform – the question of agency'. In C. Teelken, E. Ferlie and M. Dent (eds) *Leadership in the Public Sector: Promises and Pitfalls*. London: Routledge: 237–251.

Flood, J. (2011) 'The re-landscaping of the legal profession: Large law firms and professional re-regulation'. *Current Sociology*, 59 (4): 507–529.

Ford, C. (2008) 'New governance, compliance and principles-based securities regulation'. *American Business Law Journal*, 45(1): 1–60.

Foucault, M. (1979) 'On governmentality'. *Ideology & Consciousness*, 6: 5–22.

Fournier, V. (1999) 'The appeal of "professionalism" as a disciplinary mechanism'. *The Sociological Review*, 47 (2): 280–307.

Frahm, K.A. and Martin, L.L. (2009) 'From government to governance: Implications for social work administration'. *Administration in Social Work*, 33 (4): 407–422.

Freidson, E. (1994) *Professionalism Reborn: Theory, Prophecy and Policy*. Cambridge: Policy.

Freidson, E. (2001) *Professionalism: The Third Logic*. Cambridge: Polity Press.

Garrett, P. M. (2004) '"Have you seen my assessment schedule?": Proceduralisation, constraint and control in social work with children and families'. In M. Dent, J. Chandler and J. Barry (eds) *Questioning the New Public Management*. Aldershot: Ashgate: 55–70.

Goodman, R. and Peng, I. (1996) 'The East Asian Welfare States: Peripatetic learning, adaptive change, and nation-building'. In G. Esping-Andersen (ed) *Welfare States in Transition: National Adaptions in Global Economies*. London: Sage:192–224.

Gray, M. and Webb, S.A. (2013) 'Towards a "new politics" of social work'. In M. Gray and S.A. Webb (eds) *The New Politics of Social Work*. Basingstoke: Palgrave Macmillan: 3–20.

Greenwood, R., Hining, C.R. and Brown, J. (1990) '"P2 form" strategic management: Corporate practices in professional practices'. *Academy of Management Journal*, 33 (4): 725–755.

Greenwood, R. and Hinings, C.R. (1993) 'Understanding strategic change: The contribution of archetypes'. *Academy of Management Journal*, 36: 1052–1081.

Greve, B. (ed) (2013) *The Routledge Handbook of the Welfare State*. London: Routledge.

Halliwell, N. (2008) 'Encounters with medical professionals: A crisis of trust or a matter of respect?'. *Medicine, Healthcare and Philosophy*, 11 (4): 427–437.

Hood, C. (1991) 'A public management for all seasons'. *Public Administration*, 69 (1): 3–19.

Hood, C. (1995) 'The "new public management" in the 1980s: Variations on a theme'. *Accounting, Organizations and Society*, 20 (2/3): 93–109.

Jamous, H. and Peloille, B. (1970) 'Professions or self-perpetuating systems? Changes in the French university-hospital system'. In J.A. Jackson (ed) *Professions and Professionalization*. Cambridge: Cambridge University Press: 109–152.

Johnson, T. (1995) 'Governmentality and the institutionalization of expertise'. In T. Johnson, G. Larkin and M. Saks (eds) *Health Professions and the State in Europe*. London: Routledge: 7–24.

Kirkpatrick, I. (2016) 'Hybrid management and professional leadership'. In M. Dent, I.L. Bourgeault, J.-L. Denis and E. Kuhlmann (eds) *The Routledge Companion to the Professions and Professionalism*. London: Routledge: 175–187.

Kirkpatrick, I., Jespersen, P. K., Dent, M. and Neogy, I. (2009) 'Medicine and management in a comparative perspective: The case of Denmark and England'. *Sociology of Health & Illness*, 11(5): 642–658.

Kirkpatrick, I. and Noordegraaf, M. (2015) 'Organizations and occupations: towards hybrid professionalism in professional service firms?' In L. Empson, D. Muzio J. Broschak and B. Hinings (eds) *The Oxford Handbook of Professional Service Firms*. Oxford: Oxford University Press: 92–112.

Klein, R. (2001) *The New Politics of the NHS*. Harlow: Pearson Education/Prentice Hall.

Li, B. (2013) 'Welfare state changes in China since 1949'. In B. Greve (ed) *The Routledge Handbook of the Welfare State*. London: Routledge: 222–231.

Light, D. (1995) 'Countervailing powers: a framework for professions in transition'. In T. Johnson, G. Larkin and M. Saks (eds) *Health Professions and the State in Europe*. London: Routledge: 25–41.

Lipsky, M. (1980) *Street-Level Bureaucracy: Dilemmas of the Individual in Public Services*. New York: Russell Sage Foundation.

Lipsky, M. (2010) *Street-Level Bureaucracy: Dilemmas of the Individual in Public Services* (Updated edition). New York: Russell Sage Foundation.

Lloyd-Bostock, S.M. and Hunter, B.M. (2008) 'Reforming regulation of the medical profession: The risks of risk-based approaches'. *Health, Risk & Society*, 10 (1): 69–83.

Macdonald, K.M (1995) *The Sociology of the Professions*. London: Sage.

Maltby, J. (2008) 'There is no such thing as audit society1: A reading of Power'. Paper presented at the *Conference of Practical Criticism in the Managerial Social Sciences*. Leicester University Management School (January 15th–17th). Accessed via Google Scholar.

Martin, G.P. and Waring, J. (2018) 'Realising governmentality: Pastoral power, governmental discourse and the (re)constitution of subjectivities'. *The Sociological Review*, 66 (6): 1292–1308.

Meyer, J.W. and Rowan, B. (1991) 'Institutionalized organizations: Formal structure as myth and ceremony'. In W.W. Powell and P.J. DiMaggio (eds) *The New Institutionalism in Organizational Analysis*. Chicago and London: The University of Chicago Press: 41–62.

Miller, P. and Rose, N. (2008) *Governing the Present: Administering Economic, Social and Personal Life*. Cambridge: Polity

Muzio, D. and Ackroyd, S. (2008) 'Changes in the legal profession: Professional agency and the legal labour process'. In D. Muzio, S. Ackroyd and J.-F. Chanlat (eds) *Redirections in the Study of Expert Labour*. Basingstoke: Palgrave: 31–51.

Muzio, D., Ackroyd, S., and Chanlat, J.-F. (2008) 'Introduction: lawyers, doctors and business consultants'. In D. Muzio, S. Ackroyd and J.-F. Chanlat (eds) *Redirections in the Study of Expert Labour*. Basingstoke: Palgrave: 1–28.

Muzio, D., Aulakh, S. and Kirkpatrick, I. (2019) 'Professional occupations and organizations'. In R. Greenwood and N. Philips (eds) *Elements of Organization Theory* (Cambridge e-book series). Cambridge: Cambridge University Press.

Muzio, D. and Kirkpatrick, I. (eds) (2011) 'Reconnecting professional occupations and professional organizations'. *Current Sociology*, 59 (4): Monograph 2.

Nakashima, M., Chapin, R.K., Macmillan, K., and Zimmerman, M. (2005) 'Decision making in long-term care: Approaches used by older adults and implications for social work practice'. *Journal of Gerontological Social Work*, 43 (4): 79–102.

Newman, J. (2001) *Modernising Governance: New Labour, Policy and Society*. London: Sage.

Osborne, S. (2006) 'The new public governance'. *Public Management Review*, 8 (3): 377–387.

Osborne, S. (ed) (2010) *The New Public Governance?* London: Routledge.

Ouchi, W.G. (1991) 'Markets, bureaucracies and clans'. In G. Thompson, J. Frances, R. Levacic and J. Mitchell (eds) *Markets, Hierarchies & Networks: The Coordination of Social Life*. London: Sage: 246–255.

Payne, M. (2000) 'The politics of case management and social work'. *International Journal of Social Welfare*, 9: 82–91.

Pease, B. (2013) 'A history of critical and radical social work'. In M. Gray and S.A. Webb (eds) *The New Politics of Social Work*. Basingstoke: Palgrave Macmillan: 21–43.

Pierre, J. (2000) 'Introduction: Understanding governance'. In J. Pierre (ed) *Debating Governance: Authority, Steering, and Democracy*. Oxford: Oxford University Press: 1–10.

Pollitt, C. and Bouckaert, G. (2017) *Public Management Reform: A Comparative Analysis – into the Age of Austerity*. Oxford: Oxford University Press.

Powell, M.J., Brock, D.M. and Hinings, C.R. (1999) 'The changing professional organization'. In D. Brock, M. Powell and C.R. Hinings (eds) *Restructuring the Professional Organization: Accounting, Health Care and Law*. London: Routledge: 1–19.

Powell, W.W. and DiMaggio, P.J. (1991) *The New Institutionalism in Organizational Analysis*. Chicago and London: The University of Chicago Press.

Rhodes, R.A.W. (1996) 'The new governance: Governing without government'. *Political Studies*, 44: 652–667.

Rogowski, S. (2010) *Social Work: The Rise and Fall of a Profession?* Bristol: Policy Press.

Saks, M. (2017) 'A review of theories of professions, organizations and society: The case for neo-Weberianism, neo-institutionalism and eclecticism'. *Journal of Professions and Organizations*, 3: 170–187.

Salter, B. (2004) *The New Politics of Medicine*. Basingstoke: Palgrave Macmillan.

Saxonberg, S. (2013) 'Eastern Europe'. In B. Greve (ed) *The Routledge Handbook of the Welfare State*. London: Routledge: 171–182.

Saxonberg, S. and Sirovátka, T. (2009) 'Neo-liberalism by decay? The evaluation of the Czech welfare state'. *Social Policy & Administration*, 43 (2): 186–203.

Sheaff, R., Rogers, A., Pickard, S. et al. (2003) 'A subtle governance: "soft" medical leadership in English primary care'. *Sociology of Health & Illness*, 25 (5): 408–428.

Thompson, G., Frances, J., Levacic, R. and Mitchell, J. (1991) *Markets, Hierarchies & Networks: The Coordination of Social Life*. London: Sage/Open University.

Tuohy, C.H. (2012) 'Reform and the politics of hybridization in mature health care states'. *Journal of Health Economics, Policy and Law*, 37 (4): 611–632.
Verbeeten, F. H. M. and Speklé, R. F. (2015) 'Management control, results-oriented culture and public sector performance: Empirical evidence on new public management'. *Organization Studies*, 36 (7): 953–978.
Webb, S. (2002) 'Evidence-based practice and decision analysis in social work: An implementation model'. *Journal of Social Work*, 2 (1):45–63.
Webb, S.A. (2006) *Social Work in a Risk Society: Social and Political Perspectives*. Basingstoke: Palgrave Macmillan.
Weick, K.E. (1976) 'Educational organizations as loosely coupled systems'. *Administrative Science Quarterly*, 21: 1–19.
Williamson, O. E. (2002) 'The theory of the firm as governance structure: From choice to contract'. *Journal of Economic Perspectives*, 16 (3): 171–195.
Witz, A. (1992) *Professions and Patriarchy*. London: Routledge.
Worsley, A., Beddoe, L., McLaughlin, K. and Teater, B. (2020) 'Regulation, registration and social work: An international comparison'. *The British Journal of Social Work*, 50 (2): 308–325.

5 Professions, management and leadership

Introduction

In this chapter the topics to be covered are professional hybridisation, leadership and user involvement as they relate to management. Each represents an ambivalence in the relationship between professionals and management. Hybridisation involves professionals directly within management but can compromise their professional commitments, leadership may be seen in a similar light, while user involvement, which can take several forms, may *imply* greater controls over the professionals (e.g. where the client is transmuted into the consumer) although where the emphasis is on co-production the client is cast more as an ally and, perhaps, more likely to further empower the professional. In transforming themselves to accommodate to the neo-liberal realities the professions have variously adapted to new forms of management arrangements. Those in the private sector largely moved to the more corporate model of the professional service firm – and away from the classic partnership model. Those within the public sector have negotiated different approaches to working with or within management in 'hybrid' forms. However, with the shifting emphasis from managerialism towards governance (see Chapter 4) there has also been a shift in the discourse away from 'management' towards 'leadership'. This is to some extent simply rhetoric; leadership looks far more compatible with collegiality and professionalism than managerialism could ever be. Nevertheless, as Reed (2016) and O'Reilly and Reed (2011) have argued, the leadership discourse has itself been driven by the 'neo-liberal turn' (Reed 2016: 202–204) with the economic and political pressures this put on the professions within the public sector. It is particularly, but not only, within the public sector that the issue of user involvement has become increasingly important (Dent 2018). Intended to establish a forum for deliberative engagement between users (patients and carers), managers and professionals it reflected a broader democratic movement in the 1990s (Newman 2001: 130). This came to sit alongside the already-established policy of client as consumer that had been introduced in the previous decade (ibid.). These were later joined by the co-production variety of involvement, a variety even more directly with the work of the professionals than the others.

DOI: 10.4324/9780429430831-5

Whether hybrid management and leadership, along with user involvement, favours the interests of the professions or management is the topic of this chapter. To carry out this assessment the chapter reviews the range of hybrids and leadership models internationally as well as the growth of professional service firms and the implications for professions and professionalism in the coming decades. It is also important to look at the issues of management and leadership in a comparative context. In broad terms, public sector professionals across much of Western Europe have had long experience in management and leadership in ways not reflected within the UK or much of North America (Bode and Maerker 2014: 398). I am thinking here of the tradition within many countries of hospital leaders being people with medical backgrounds (Dent, Kirkpatrick and Neogy 2012: 105–125). Similarly, across the old state socialist countries of Russia and Eastern Europe (Pollitt and Bouckhaert 2017: 62). On the other hand, in the case of private sector professionals the opposite would appear to be the case. Here the corporatisation of professional practices appears to have emanated primarily from within the USA for reasons largely relating to the result of 'the deregulation of professional markets and increased competition, financial constraints and cost pressures, changes in government policies, globalization and the demands of international clients, increasingly sophisticated clients and technological change' (Powell, Brock and Hinings 1999: 9). All this led to the creation and international spread of professional services firms (PSFs) (Hinings 2016: 166–168; Muzio, Aulakh and Kirkpatrick 2019; Empson, Muzio, Broschak and Hinings 2015). The driver for the changes within the public sector was the parallel neo-liberal reforms of the 1980s – if not before – that led to the growing marketisation and managerialisation across the public sector with the widespread introduction of New Public Management (NPM) (Dent and Barry 2004; Pollitt and Bouckaert 2017). Within the public sector NPM (Hood 1991, 1995) there was a widespread concern that the prioritisation of the efficiency of the markets would be at the expense of civic values (Hood 1991: 16). Some countries embraced NPM more readily than others, so UK and Sweden were early converts while Germany was not. Nevertheless, even Germany eventually succumbed with the adoption of a modified version of NPM, at least within several city states and *Länder* at the end of the twentieth century. This version was known as the new steering model (*Das Neues Steuerungmodell*) and was based on the Dutch Tilburg model (Pollitt and Bouckaert 2017: 296; Dent, Howarth, Mueller and Preuschoft 2004).

NPM for many professionals was an anathema. It was contrary to their sense of professionalism. Clients and patients were, formally at least, converted into consumers and the response from the professions was not one of universal approval. However, many public sector professionals were more ambivalent than hostile (Numerato, Salvatore and Fattore 2012; Llewellyn 2001). Indeed, some health care organisations, especially in Scandinavia, took to ensuring their senior doctors received good management training as

Kirkpatrick and colleagues' Danish study has shown (Kirkpatrick, Jespersen, Dent and Neogy 2009; Kirkpatrick, Dent and Jespersen 2011). The training was largely welcomed by the medics because it gave them a real sense of ascendancy within the organisation, similar in some ways to that they had enjoyed historically. Similar developments have occurred across Europe and the Anglophone world although not always experienced as positively as that by the Danish hospital doctors (Bode and Dent 2014). This management training reflects a more general process of managerial incorporation of the medical profession – a process commonly referred to as *hybridisation.*

Hybrids and hybridisation

The challenge for professionals involved in management is how one can be credible professionally if you are spending time also being a manager. And equally important, how can one maintain the trust of colleagues if as a manager one has, possibly, a different set of values? There are a variety of answers to these questions generally of a pragmatic kind reflecting a path dependency such that the solutions for English hospital doctors, for example, will be somewhat different to those adopted in, say, Germany (Dent, Kirkpatrick and Neogy 2012; Bode and Maerker 2014; Bode and Dent 2014; Dent, Howorth, Mueller and Preuschoft 2004). The term that has come to be used for such professionals is 'hybrid' as they reflect the 'recombination of existing elements [professional and organisational] often in tension' (Kirkpatrick 2016: 175). In other words, the experience of becoming a 'hybrid' for professionals tends to be one of ambivalence and uncertainty (Noordegraaf 2007) and maybe but a transitional state (Noordegraaf 2015).

Early in the adoption of the NPM reforms the taking on managerial responsibilities as a professional was often seen as somehow unprofessional. 'Going over to the dark side' is a common ironic comment often heard, for example, within the medical profession. Over time, however, these roles have become normalised and are associated with widespread changes across professional work organisations. There tends to be some variation between the more autonomous professions including medicine and law and those professions more dependent upon the state for employment and clients. Examples of the latter would include nurses and social workers (Kirkpatrick 2016: 179). An important development here has been the restratification of professional organisations, which goes beyond Freidson's (1985, 1994) thesis on the subject. While Freidson's 'administrative elites' within the professions may see the defence of professional interests as part of their managerial role (Freidson 1994: 142; Kirkpatrick 2016: 177), the reality happens to be more complex. Restratification marked one of the first steps in the reconfiguration of professional organisations and one that would radically reshape what it means to be a professional. Moreover, restratification, as Kirkpatrick (2016: 177–180) points out, represents, broadly, two modes of differentiation of the hybrid professional-manager role: vertical stratification and horizontal. In the case of *vertical stratification* Causer and Exworthy (1999: 84–85) suggest the following categories:

1 Hybrid professional-manager
2 Quasi-managerial practitioners
3 General full-time managers

These categories are very general, but nevertheless useful, for they enable us to distinguish between, for example, doctors or nurses with ward or departmental management responsibilities alongside their clinical duties. Whereas the role of a hospital medical director might well be either a quasi-managerial practitioner or a full-time manager – depending on whether the person is continuing to retain any clinics of their own – and one can identify parallel arrangements within PSFs too (Kirkpatrick 2016: 176). Even the full-time manager, who is also a qualified and previously practicing professional, reflects 'hybridity' because their role is dependent on their professional knowledge to provide the authority for their leadership. Within nursing, teaching and social work, managerial roles are now structured as part of the career path. This contrasts with doctors who will normally be able to decide how much clinical work to maintain alongside their managerial responsibility in order to (a) maintain collegiate credibility with their colleagues or (b) plan their future career moves (whether to move more into the managerial/corporate field or to remain true to their professional vocation). I will return to this topic later in this chapter, specifically in connection with the medical profession within a comparative context.

Horizontal differentiation is a more general phenomenon, well established among the more traditional and autonomous professions such as law and accountancy as well as medicine, but rather less so among the organisational professions of nursing, teaching and social work. These latter professions, with their less well-developed independent occupational culture (Kirkpatrick, Ackroyd and Walker 2005), have long-established hybrid-managerial roles within their career structures. Doctors, by contrast, traditionally have had far greater opportunities and rewards for private practice, clinical research and have had a later and more ambivalent attitude to engaging in more hybrid roles associated with managerial activities (Kirkpatrick 2016: 179; Llewellyn 2001; Numerato, Salvatore and Fattore 2012). Similar developments have occurred within other more private sector professions, including accountancy and law, which is coming up next.

The corporate (private sector) approach

For many of the twentieth-century professional organisations, whether in the public or private sector, required only a limited managerial function to coordinate the work and ensure sufficiently its quality (Mintzberg 1983: 189). This was the arrangement that underpinned the professional partnership, which until the second half of the twentieth century characterised most professional organisations in the private sector. These professional partnerships – P^2 organisations as Greenwood, Hining and Brown (1990) categorised them – are collegiate, knowledge-intensive, organisations characterised by a strong client focus, individual autonomy for the partners and consensus-based peer control (Hinings, Greenwood and Cooper 1999: 134). In these organisations managerial hybrids have not been particularly in evidence. However, many professional organisations, particularly, accountancy and law firms, have grown and extended into global operations, along with management consultancies and professional services firms (PSFs) (Greenwood, Hinings and Prakash 2017: 114) and these can hardly be viewed as simple partnerships. The proponents of the P^2 organisational type recognised them as having more in common with corporate organisations and named them Managed Professional Businesses (MPBs) (Hinings, Greenwood and Cooper 1999: 130). This nomenclature reflected not only the growth of the organisations but their increased focus on effectiveness and efficiency (Hinings, Greenwood and Cooper 1999: 134). The development led to an erosion of the qualities of the P^2 (partnership) archetype and a shift in emphasis on hybridisation (Muzio, Aulakh, and Kirkpatrick 2019).

This archetype, or configuration, as Greenwood and Hinings (1993) preferred, we think of professional organisations (Powell, Brock and Hinings 1999: 3), grew more evident towards the latter end of the twentieth century. This was in the wake of neo-liberalism and the opportunities it presented. Its growth paralleled that of NPM in the public sector and was global (Muzio, Aulakh and Kirkpatrick 2019). This has presented challenges for traditional models of collegiate professionalism, although there is evidence of its continued survival albeit in a reconfigured and diluted form (Adler, Kwon and Heckscher 2008; Noordegraaf 2011). All of this suggests that the professions affected are adapting their professionalism to the new realities of managerialism and organisational controls, but in ways that indicate an even greater symbiosis between the professions and the MPBs (including PSFs) than previously. Within organisational studies, a major focus of research interest from the 1990s was the professional services firms (PSFs). While the P^2 paper (Greenwood, Hining and Brown 1990) has continued to be a touchstone for many researchers in this field, PSF research reflects some key differences. First, P^2 research identifies partnership ownership and collegiate governance as crucial (Greenwood, Hinings and Prakash 2017) and the analyses of MPBs appear to be adopting the same archetypal template; however, this is not universally the case in the study of PSFs. von Nordenflycht (2010), for a key example, highlights (1) knowledge intensity, (2) low capital intensity and (3) a professionalised workforce as the distinctive characteristics of PSFs. One of the reasons for this is the range and variety of firms and expertise covered by the umbrella term PSF. Initially, the P^2 archetype was applied to accounting firms and relatively soon after was extended to law firms and management consultancy firms (Greenwood, Hinings and Prakash 2017: 114). Then other researchers concentrated on 'knowledge-intensive' organisations regardless of their ownership arrangements (Seabrook 2014) and one will find a wide variety of firms included under this rubric. von Nordenflycht (2010: 165–167) suggests a fourfold typology in an attempt to draw some boundaries. These are as follows, with examples:

1 Classic – or regulated – PSFs: law, accounting and architecture
2 Professional campuses: hospitals
3 Neo-PSFs: consulting, advertising
4 Technology developers: biotechnology, R&D laboratories

Starting at the top, the 'classic PSFs' (1) have the highest degree of professional services intensity. The 'professional campuses' (2) are similar in sharing, to a large extent, professional services intensity, but it is also characterised by a high level of capital intensity. The next two categories have far less professional services intensity but share a high knowledge intensity; 'neo-PSFs' (3) are so labelled because they have a weakly professionalised, or even a non-professionalised, workforce; by contrast, the 'technology developers' (4) employ professional engineers and scientists, but this is not reflected in professional services intensity given the way the work is organised in that there is far less a distinctive client focus but it does reflect high, or relatively high, technology intensity.

The managerial challenge, which von Nordenflycht (2010) unoriginally identifies as like 'herding cats', results from the workforce being intellectually skilled with high labour market value and which is committed to working autonomously. In this context, management requires a particular mix of incentives and control systems. Classically, this would have involved the expectation of becoming a partner, ensuring a matching of individual incentives and values and the firm's interests. This, however, is not an option in the case of most PSFs. Here the control systems are more the responsibility of hybrid professional-managers, or even specialist managers (Muzio, Aulakh and Kirkpatrick 2019: 65), and this is further reinforced with the introduction of accountability systems, such as computerised time-management billing systems (Muzio, Aulakh and Kirkpatrick 2019: 65; Campbell and Charlesworth 2012).

In terms of managerialism, there is more in common between the public and private sectors than might be supposed. Perhaps, that should not be too surprising given that one of the central principles of NPM was for the public sector to emulate the private. Nevertheless, it is important to keep in mind that, while professionals in both sectors are generally attempting to defend their occupational jurisdictions, the rationale of managerialism is *not* precisely the same across the two sectors as only in one (private) is it completely market driven. In the private sector hybridisation of professional roles appears to be viewed by the participants as less of a challenge than in the public sector, in part because it reflects the opportunities of business growth (Muzio, Aulakh and Kirkpatrick 2019: 56). If a lawyer or accountant, for example, prefers not to work within one of the corporate PSFs they will have the opportunity to work within a P^2 partnership or perhaps even go into solo practice. Not so, or not to the same extent, for example, in the case of doctors or social workers. Over the same period, the management discourse has increasingly turned its attention to the issue of leadership and particularly so within the public sector.

Leadership

Perhaps the central question around the discourse of leadership here is how far does it reflect a recovery of professional autonomy from the new managerialism. I say 'perhaps', because the leadership discourse in the post-NPM era may be, in part, an ideological one giving rise to the concept of 'leaderism' (O'Reilly and Reed 2012: 22). This Reed (2016) described as providing the imagery for combining neo-liberal ideology and professional autonomy to create a 'hybridized form of polyarchic governance' (Reed 2016: 210) that would appeal to professional actors at a time when a management identity – along with managerialism – appeared to be losing its appeal (Carroll and Levy 2008). From this viewpoint the growing emphasis on leadership results from the relative failure of managerialism to implement the policy priorities (Reed 2016: 2010). In the UK, leadership and professionalism emerged in the 1990s as a key theme. Its intended purpose was to transform public services into dynamic, innovative enterprises (Reed 2016: 201) and overcome the limitations of NPM. It involved encouraging elements within the professions taking on a 'responsibilised' leadership role; getting professionals to become champions of particular policies and willing to work in interdisciplinary ways to bring about change (Dent, Kirkpatrick and Neogy 2012: 120; Martin and Learmonth 2012). Initially, there was much discussion around the need for *transformational* leadership as opposed to the *transactional* type that characterises the NPM technologies of audit and performance targets. This distinction broadly reflects the Weberian distinction between '*charismatic*' and '*legal-rational*' authority, although this was too simplistic as policy innovations tend to be complex requiring detailed collaboration across professional and managerial disciplines. Whether this reconfiguration of professions' intra-relations and inter-relations is negative or positive for the professions is a moot point (Denis, Gestel and Lepage 2016: 215–216). What is clear is that all organised professions have had to adapt – or 'mutate' to use Adler and Kwon's 2013 terminology – to the changing realities. Take one example from health care, the one utilised by Adler and Kwon (2013) that of *clinical guidelines* (see Chapter 4, where the topic is treated from a governance perspective). These are generally constructed according to evidence-based methods that the medical profession is happy with on the grounds that they are scientifically fairly rigorous. Similar use is made of guidelines and protocols within other professions including law, as discussed in Chapter 4. Within medicine they are also a component part of *integrated care pathways* (ICPs), which are 'multidisciplinary care management tools [that] map out chronologically key activities in a healthcare process' (Allen 2009: 354). They enable considerable external monitoring and audit of health care work (including medicine). Nursing has been successful in taking the leadership of care pathway developments (Allen 2009: 355), doctors have been far more equivocal. Partly because care pathways, as opposed to clinical guidelines, fail to meet the scientific rigour that clinical guidelines are assumed to have undergone (Allen 2014). The implicit, and additional, medical concern is that care pathways could be used as a vehicle for undermining their ascendancy within the health care division of labour. By comparison, clinical guidelines are more securely under the medical professions' control, for it is the doctors who have the pre-eminent role in establishing their criteria. As McDonald and Harrison (2004) demonstrated it is not the clinical guidelines themselves that undermine medical and clinical autonomy, but how they are implemented. Nursing, by contrast, has been the profession that has explicitly championed ICPs as an important way of advancing its status and influence (Allen 2014: 812). This is on the grounds that by showing leadership in the adoption and implementation of the guidelines that feed into ICPs they have established a basis for their own professional autonomy in the post-NPM era. It is an important way of working with management and, increasingly importantly, patients and carers in collaborative ways. This autonomy is much more professionally collectivist than previously and involves accepting some budgetary constraints and preparedness to contemplate the need for organisational efficiencies (clinical guidelines, especially when embedded within care pathways being a key example). Consequently, these developments, or 'mutations' (Adler and Kwon 2013), have not ultimately undermined the relative jurisdictional authorities of either medicine or nursing. This shift from individualistic or small group clinical autonomy to a collectivistic clinical guideline-based autonomy has involved leadership, but not primarily of the transformative kind. Although medicine is never short of potential charismatic leaders, the diffusion of clinical guidelines was much more dependent upon *distributed* (Day, Gronn and Salas 2004; Gronn 2002) or *collective* leadership (Denis, Lamothe and Langley 2001). This is where many – but certainly not all – within the profession play an active part in creating and maintaining the ground rules for professional practice, for example, in establishing and maintaining clinical guidelines in their day-to-day usage. There is one remaining element of this jigsaw that needs consideration, and that is the issue of the particularities of history and culture, of path dependency.

Path dependency

Management and leadership, like much else, are embedded within organisational and societal cultures, and are path dependent (Peters, Pierre and King 2005; Tuohy 1999:260–261; Wilsford 1994). There is a literature on cultural patterns of leadership internationally, perhaps best-known being Hofstede (1980, 1991), which in turn stimulated the subsequent GLOBE study (House, Hanges, Javidan, Dorman and Gupta 2004). In addition to not being particularly about the professions, they also tend to provide a macroscopic perspective and lack the processual elements of leadership. Better then to turn our attention elsewhere, namely path dependency. This is so even if at first sight it does not look that promising, for as Wilsford (1994) has pointed out – with reference to the French health system and its professionals – it is the *status quo* that characterises path dependency. It is so deeply embedded that it needs a crisis to bring about any fundamental change. A crisis is needed to force a conjunction of diverse elements into a new single combination that can reconfigure relationships (Wilsford 1994: 257). More prosaically pathway dependence can be viewed as being 'sticky', in the sense 'that particular courses of actions, once introduced, can be virtually impossible to reverse' (Pierson 1997). Nevertheless, path dependency happens to best describe the changes within the professions in the wake of neo-liberalism.

DiMaggio and Powell (1991), discussing the propensity for organisational change from a New Institutionalist perspective, suggest that this would only occur *coercively, mimetically* or *normatively*. This approach has been widely accepted within the organisational studies literature although less so within the sociology of professions, but what these two related approaches offer is a template for the international comparison of the professions and the impact of managerialism and possibly the new wave of leadership or 'leaderism' (Reed 2016; O'Reilly and Reed 2011). To be more concrete here, the biggest conjuncture relevant to this discussion, that hit western economies, was the post-war recessions of the 1970s that played a significant part in the rise of the Reagan administration in the USA and that of Thatcher in the UK. They marked the fall from grace for Keynesian, which, in the post-war period, underpinned the rationale for much of the work and influence of the professions in the public sector. Now in the 1970s and the 1980s the neo-liberalism of Hayek (Boston 2013: 18–19; Rollings 2013: 637–638) was firmly on the agenda. As a consequence, the professions came in for far more political criticism than previously (Burrage 1992: 1). To take just one example, the 1989 reform of the legal profession in the UK, in order 'to ensure that the public was provided with the most efficient and effective network of legal services at the most economical price' (Zander 1990: 758). In policy terms what impacted most on the public sector professions, however, was the emergence of what became known as New Public Management (NPM) (discussed in Chapter 4) (Pollitt and Bouckaert 2017; Dent, Chandler and Barry 2004; Hood 1991). An approach to organising and delivering public services that through greater emphasis on performance and other 'hard' measures or on 'softer' ones of quality and customer satisfaction (Ferlie and Geraghty 2005) brought about a shift away from professional control and towards management.

In addition to the hybridisation debate discussed earlier, NPM also raised the question as to whether it would become the universal template in the West. It is this issue of its international diffusion and isomorphism in the face of path dependency and the implications for any general institutional convergence to which this chapter now concerns itself, particularly in relation to the public sector professions. Here the focus will primarily – but not exclusively – be on the medical profession, a topic I know reasonably well. The widely accepted assumption has been that NPM would be diffused throughout the world, but this view is oversimplistic. Any tendency towards global convergence has been offset by considerable variation and the complications of 'other reforms and combinations of reforms' (Pollitt and Bouckaert 2017: 11). This not only influenced the pattern of public management but that of the work of the professions too. Indeed, it would often be the peculiar institutional history of the professions that would substantially dictate the extent and efficacy of NPM adoption within a country and/or sector (Dent 2003a; Dent, Kirkpatrick and Neogy 2012). There has, moreover, often been a difference between the decision to adopt administrative reforms including NPM and their implementation (Pollitt and Bouckaert 2017: 32–44). At each stage from initial interest through adoption and then outcome the process becomes increasingly complex in the face of the necessary negotiations with key players and the interplay with other competing reforms or practices (Tuohy 1999; Denis, Germain, Regis and Veronisi 2021). Differences are especially noticeable between Anglophone and mainland European countries, the latter typically identified as 'corporate' or 'conservative' (Esping-Andersen 1999: 81–86) and having strong 'Napoleonic tradition' (Pollitt and Bouckaert 2017: 12). This is somewhat different from the liberal traditions of the Anglophones.

In the case of medicine there are a range of comparative studies of medical management and leadership studies that cover several European countries and the USA including Kirkpatrick, Kuhlmann, Hartley, Dent and Lega (2016); Bode and Dent (2014); Dent, Kirkpatrick and Neogy (2012); and Kirkpatrick, Dent and Jespersen (2011). These provide a good basis for examining comparative variations in medical management and leadership. The focus here will be on the acute hospital sector, given this is where the power of the medical profession has historically been concentrated and where it has been questioned the most (Kirkpatrick, Jespersen, Dent and Neogy 2009: 645). This has been as much on the grounds of quality of care and clinical governance (Salter 2004) as the demands of patient and public involvement (Dent 2018; Dent and Pahor 2015). Both influence the character of managerial rationalisation in the different countries as will be touched upon later in this chapter.

Hybrids revisited

Within medicine, as with other professions, assumptions of collegiality have been increasingly challenged by stratification. Freidson (1994: 142–143) posits three strata: 'rank and file'; 'knowledge elite'; and 'administrative elite' which correspond in terms of hospital doctors, those involved with direct patient care, those involved in research and education and those involved in administration and management. To an extent most doctors will have involved themselves with two of these, possibly as hospital doctors (rank and file) with administrative responsibilities (administrative) or as academic researchers with some clinical work (knowledge). These 'strata' have long existed although the administrative element would have not been 'highly elaborated' (Mintzberg 1983: 194). Some of the knowledge and administrative roles would clearly be recognised as elite status at least up until the introduction of NPM as Jespersen and Wrede (2009), for example, have reported in the case of the Nordic countries. More generally, however, the administrative roles were seen as routine and reflected more of a collegiate responsibility. What has changed was the growth of managerialism (NPM), which has – realistically – been interpreted as an attempt to subordinate hospital doctors to management qua management control in the interests of greater efficiency and economy. This initially challenged the professionals but over time the profession has negotiated and adapted such that they have established a newer form of 'medical ascendancy', that is, one in a reconfigured form (Dent and Barry 2004). This has possibly given rise to a new professionalism as Evetts (2011) has argued, or a connective one as Noordegraaf (2015, 2020) has suggested. In the latter 'connective' case, it is one that has 'to be generated, reproduced, co-produced, redesigned and deserved – an active process' (Noordegraaf 2020: 7). This is after hybridity, where medical engagement in management has become normalised. While there is much in evidence that supports this argument, particularly in the case of the medical profession, it is not yet universal, as commentators on Noordegraaf's (2020) paper have argued (Adams, Kirkpatrick, Tolbert and Waring 2020b; Adams, Clegg, Eyal, Reed and Saks 2020a). Moreover, how this gets mapped out across different health care systems and regimes may well vary. These regimes are what pattern the variations in the initial 'transition from "pure" to "hybrid" professionalism' (to paraphrase Noordegraaf [2007]), across different countries. It was the Johns Hopkins model of clinical directorates (Kirkpatrick, Dent and Jespersen 2011: 496) that provided the original template that created the modern form of medical/management hybrid within health care organisations. This, however, has been extensively modified – or 'translated' – locally. As, for example, in the cases of 'medical poles' in France (Vinot 2014) and 'clusters' in the Netherlands (Dent, Kirkpatrick and Neogy 2012: 117). Every country's system has produced its own variation to the 'hybridisation' theme shaped by their particular path dependency and consequently the medical profession's response to pressures to take on managerial responsibilities. These hybrid roles, to also continue the discussion started earlier in the chapter, can take on several forms. These reflect whether they relate to departmental management or senior leadership roles. Byrkjeflot and Jespersen (2014) have usefully suggested three varieties (ideal types) of hybrid manager within health care: 1. *Clinical manager*; 2. *Commercialised manager*; 3. *Non-bureaucratic manager*. The emphasis here is a little different to that of Causer and Exworthy (1999) cited earlier, for this typology is not so much focused on hierarchy but on the range within hybridisation. Moreover, these are ideal types and like all such conceptualisations will not be found in any 'pure' form (Byrkjeflot and Jespersen 2014: 444). Nevertheless, they are both broadly and readily recognisable. Thus:

> The *clinical manager* is a hybrid role where clinicians (mostly doctors) take the role as manager but without completely leaving the professional work. In this way they mediate between the traditional logic of professional self-governance and the new general management logic inspired by NPM.
>
> (Byrkjeflot and Jespersen 2014: 445 *emphasis added*)

These *clinical managers* are the bedrock of the medical hybrids, typically staffing the clinical directorates working in a team alongside a nurse and a business manager. Certainly, that has been the model in the UK (Dent, Kirkpatrick and Neogy 2012: 112–114) and a similar pattern can be found in Scandinavian countries. Interestingly, however, nurses in Norway and Sweden have been particularly active in competing with their medical colleagues to take on hybrid management positions at the departmental (i.e. clinic) level (Byrkjeflot and Jespersen 2014: 446; Kirkpatrick, Jespersen, Dent and Neogy 2009: 649). In the Corporate and Southern European regimes (Dent 2003a: 12; Esping-Andersen 1999: 90) nursing has had a tougher struggle to gain professional recognition (Dent 2002, 2003c), and the division of labour within the hospitals and health services generally tend to reflect a strong professional apartheid between medicine and nursing, with little, if any, involvement in clinical management or in the development of specialist nursing as is commonly found in the Anglophone or Scandinavian countries. The *commercialised manager* type, by comparison, is the one who blends professionalism with an enterprise logic on behalf of management and is less common than the *clinical managers*. Although there have been some evidence of *clinical manager* hybrids exhibiting an enterprise logic within their broader responsibilities (Byrkjeflot and Jespersen (2014: 447–448), which has fluctuated depending on the broader policies of the time. But even where the entrepreneurialism culture has been dominant, for example, in New Zealand (Doolin 2002), the hospital doctors are still 'constrained by their traditional medical ethos and the need to retain professional credibility with other clinicians' (Doolin 2002: 380).

This need to retain professional credibility has worked in a peculiarly paradoxical way within one European country, namely The Netherlands, where the entrepreneurial values among hospital doctors are deep-rooted (Dent,

Kirkpatrick and Neogy 2012: 116–117). Here the implementation of NPM reforms met with strong opposition from the hospital specialists who have seen their chief role as attracting work and income to the hospital. Various reforms have been attempted (Dent 2003a) leading eventually to the emergence of 'clusters'. This has an affinity with clinical directorates except the relationship with the hospital management is a 'trading one' reflecting a stronger resistance to managerial incorporation than found elsewhere (Dent, Kirkpatrick and Neogy 2012: 116–117). There are also resonances here with the traditional notion of 'chambers' that characterises the German health care system (Dent 2003a). The final category, the *neo-bureaucratic manager*, is in some ways more amorphous than the other two, for it relates principally to governance, and more specifically to clinical governance and regulation. This all relates to the emergence of medical and clinical audits (Miller, Kurunmäki and O'leary 2008); Power 1999), performance indicators, evidence-based medicine and clinical guidelines (see Chapter 4). Instead of trusting the individual hospital doctor, one is intended to trust the governance system that the doctor inhabits. This works more along the lines of 'soft bureaucracy' (Courpasson 2000) with doctors self-monitoring their practice while being subject to regular scrutiny, for example, via staff appraisals, revalidation as well as external institutional inspections, which in England would be carried out by the Care Quality Commission (CQC). These forms of governance will vary across countries, with professional revalidation widespread across Europe (Merkur, Mossialos, Long and McKee 2008) and national quality registries (along with accreditation) that have played a more significant role in Sweden (Levay and Waks 2009). What this tends to mean is that the role of *neo-bureaucratic manager* is diffused across the profession and beyond (e.g. nurses often play an important role in developing and implementing care guidelines) (Allen 2009, 2014; Dent and Tutt 2014). Nevertheless, within hospitals, one of the key responsibilities of the medical directors is to oversee compliance to clinical governance and quality improvements (Kirkpatrick, Jespersen, Dent and Neogy 2009: 647). Other examples include those members of the profession who take part in setting up, validating and monitoring care guidelines, as well as national audits on best practice and the like, including, for instance, the National Institute for Health and Care Excellence (NICE) in the UK. This broader, somewhat disembodied leadership role of the *neo-bureaucratic manager* reflects more the 'action at a distance', a concept that Miller and Rose (2008: 33–34) borrows from Actor Network Theory. Here it can be applied to systems of clinical governance, to explain how networks of evidence-based medicine and practice, clinical guidelines and care pathways along with the requirements of regulatory regimes more generally may be held in alignment (e.g. Allen 2009). It also embodies, more concretely, the notion of distributed leadership that was mentioned earlier in the chapter (Gronn 2002; Fitzgerald, Ferlie, McGivern and Buchanan 2013). Hybrid types have their parallels within other professional organisations, although with different emphases, for example, in the case of the commercial hybrid. This will be less pronounced within social work, for example, than within one of the 'Big Four' accountancy firms (Kornberger, Justesen and Mouritsen 2011)

Management and leadership of users

Another angle to the issues of management and leadership is in relation to the service users, and clients/patients. In the case of medicine, doctors have historically *managed* patients and there are parallels with other professions too. There are two reasons for this. The first is simply to keep control over the workload and to ensure adequate income is earned. This is also true for schoolteachers and social workers as well as for lawyers and accountants even if it is less obvious in the case of the first two professions than the latter two. Put bluntly, if a school, for example, has fewer pupils than previously it is likely to employ fewer teachers. This leads to the second reason, to aid efficiency, it is useful if the professionals can socialise their 'clients' to be cooperative. Within medicine, for example, particularly for those patients with long-term or chronic illness who are regular attendees at hospital clinics, socialisation takes two forms. First, there is the direct communication and information provided by the clinics as to what the patient should expect and how they might best prepare for the next visit, examination, procedure or operation and so forth. But there is also a 'hidden curriculum' of para-professionalisation at work, which tends to inculcate 'a simplified and censored version of professional knowledge' (de Swaan 1988: 244–246). This provides the patients with a sense of understanding the medical and clinical processes and a means of communicating with the professionals. It includes all the various kinds of medical information that the patient can find on the internet and social media, even if this may be seen as a challenge by the doctors (Vinson 2016: 1370). While it appears contrary to the classic version of proto-professionalism, whereby the 'neophyte professional becomes socialized in the norms and values of a profession' (Dent 2017: 29) it, nevertheless, can simply be viewed as another variant of it. This is so even if it reflects a shift that Vinson (2016), for one, sees as evidence of the growing 'countervailing power' of patients. This version of empowerment provides the patient with the means, apparently, to discriminate in the quality of care available between different treatments, hospitals and clinics. It is important for the doctors, therefore, to ensure their version of medicine will be seen as the most convincing. A method for achieving this is now taught in medical school, as Vinson (2016: 1370) demonstrates in her study of a medical school in the USA. This more collaborative approach to gaining patient compliance also aids the medical profession in protecting its jurisdictional power from further managerial erosion. While consumer choice may well be intended to undermine established medical dominance (Dent and Pahor 2015), the co-determination variant of user involvement reshapes the asymmetric relations between medics and patients so that it appears to be based on collaboration rather than the more traditional paternalism (ibid.) even if this newer discourse is a reworking of medical paternalism similarly meant to gain patient compliance (ibid.: 547). With the increased emphasis on user involvement as part of clinical governance (Dent 2006) (see Chapter 4) the medical profession has become assiduous in ensuring they play a significant role in shaping the processes of co-production.

Conclusions

In this chapter, I have concentrated predominantly on the medical profession, as a particularly illustrative case for the three discourses of hybridisation, leadership and co-production and the impact they have had on health professionals, particularly doctors. This chapter built very much on the governance chapter that precedes it, for they are largely 'two sides of the same coin' both reflecting the ways in which professional organisations are coordinated and controlled within neo-liberalism, and after NPM. These three discourses have also impacted other professions in various ways as has been indicated as all part of neo-liberal turn and its aftermath. Now the policy emphasis is more on governance than management. The professions have shown clear signs of adapting to this new reality, and there has been a reconfiguration of the relationships between professions and organisations (Noordegraaf 2015, 2020), for example. The relationship between professionals and management has changed (and continues to change) from separation to integration. The term hybrid is perhaps less relevant for the new generations of professionals as they are less inclined to see the management and governance roles as particularly ambiguous or ambivalent. Instead, they are the 'new normal', one which provides the context for any contemporary contestation around the nature and extent of professional autonomy and ascendancy within organisations. At the same time, managerialism is a reality that has failed to be seen, or experienced, positively. In light of this, it is hardly surprising that professionals are more persuaded by the language of leadership, than management, even if this version of leadership is one that is firmly integrated into the organisation (and not the profession).

References

All internet links accessed and checked on 24 May 2023 or later.

Adams, T.L., Clegg, S., Eyal, G., Reed, M. and Saks, M. (2020a) 'Connective professionalism: towards (yet another) ideal type'. *Journal of Professions and Organizations*, 7 (2): 224–233.

Adams, T.L., Kirkpatrick, I., Tolbert, P.S. and Waring, J. (2020b) 'From protective to connective professionalism: quo vadis professional exclusivity?' *Journal of Professions and Organizations*, 7 (2): 234–245.

Adler, P.S. and Kwon, S.-W. (2013) 'The mutation of professionalism as a contested diffusion process: Clinical guidelines as carriers of institutional change in medicine'. *Journal of Management Studies*, 50 (5): 930–962.

Adler, P.S., Kwon, S.-W. and Heckscher, C. (2008) 'Professional work: The emergence of collaborative community'. *Organization Science*, 19 (2): 359–376.

Allen, D. (2009) 'From boundary concept to boundary object: The practice and politics of care pathway development'. *Social Science & Medicine*, 69: 354–361.

Allen, D. (2014) 'Lost in translation? "Evidence" and the articulation of institutional logics in integrated care pathways: From positive to negative boundary object?'. *Sociology of Health and Illness*, 36 (6): 807–822.

Bode, I. and Dent, M. (2014) 'Converging hybrid worlds? Medicine and management in Europe'. *International Journal of Public Sector Management*, 27 (5): 1–14.

Bode, I. and Maerker, M. (2014) 'Management in medicine or medics in management? The changing role of doctors in German hospitals'. *International Journal of Public Sector Management*, 27 (5): 395–405.

Boston, J. (2013) 'Basic NPM ideas and their development'. In T. Christensen and P. Lægreid (eds) *The Ashgate Research Companion to New Public Management*. Farnham: Ashgate: 17–32.

Burrage, M. (1992) 'Mrs Thatcher against deep structures: Ideology, impact and ironies of her eleven year confrontation with the professions'. Berkeley, CA: UC Berkeley Working Paper, 92–11. Available at https://escholarship.org/uc/item/74g8h37c

Byrkjeflot, H. and Jespersen, P.K. (2014) 'Three conceptualizations of hybrid management in hospitals'. *International Journal of Public Sector Management*, 27 (5): 441–458.

Campbell, I. and Charlesworth, S. (2012) 'Salaried lawyers and billable hours: a new perspective from the sociology of work'. *International Journal of the Legal Profession*, 19 (1): 89–122.

Carroll, B. and Levy, L. (2008) 'Defaulting to management: Leadership defined by what it is not'. *Organization*, 15 (1): 75–96.

Causer, G. and Exworthy, M. (1999) 'Professionals and managers across the public sector'. In M. Exworthy and S. Halford (eds) *Professionals and the New Managerialism in the Public Sector*. Buckingham: Open University.

Courpasson, D. (2000) 'Managerial strategies of domination, power in soft bureaucracies'. *Organization Studies*, 21 (1): 141–161.

Day, D., Gronn, P. and Salas, E. (2004) 'Leadership capacity in teams'. *Leadership Quarterly*, 15 (6): 857–880.

Denis, J.-L., Germain, S., Regis, C. and Veronisi, G. (2022) *The Role of Medical Doctors in Health Reforms: A Comparative Analysis of Canada and England*. Bristol: Policy Press.

Denis, J-L., van Gestel, N. and Lepage, A. (2016) 'Professional agency, leadership and organizational change'. In M. Dent, I.V. Bourgeault, J-L. Denis and E. Kuhlmann (eds) *The Routledge Companion to the Professions and Professionalism*. London: Routledge: 215–227.

Denis, J.-L., Lamothe, L. and Langley, A. (2001) 'The dynamics of collective leadership and strategic change in pluralistic organizations'. *Academy of Management Journal*, 33 (4): 809–837.

Dent, M. (2002) 'Professional predicaments: Comparing the professionalisation projects of German and Italian nurses'. *International Journal of Public Sector Management*, 15 (2): 151–162.

Dent, M. (2003a) *Remodelling Hospitals and Health Professions in Europe: Medicine, Nursing and the State*. Basingstoke: Palgrave.

Dent, M. (2003c) 'Polish and Greek Nursing: Gender, Familialism and Clientelism'. *International Journal of Public Sector Management*, 16 (2): 153–162.

Dent, M. (2006) 'Disciplining the medical profession? Implications of patient choice for medical dominance'. *Health Sociology Review*, 15 (5): 458–468.

Dent, M. (2017) 'Perspectives on professional identity'. In S.A. Webb (ed) *Professional Identity and Social Work*. London: Routledge: 21–34.

Dent, M. (2018) 'Health care governance, user involvement and medical regulation in Europe'. In J.M. Chamberlain, M. Dent and M. Saks (eds) *Professional Health Regulation in the Public Interest: International perspectives*. Bristol: Policy Press: 17–37.

Dent, M. and Barry, J. (2004) 'New public management and the professions in the UK: Reconfiguring control?'. In M. Dent, J. Chandler and J. Barry (eds) *Questioning the New Public Management*. Aldershot: Ashgate: 7–20.

Dent, M., Chandler, J. and Barry, J. (eds) (2004) *Questioning the New Public Management*. Aldershot: Ashgate.

Dent, M., Howorth, C., Mueller, F. and Preuschoft, C. (2004) 'Archetype transition in the German health service? The attempted modernisation of hospitals in a north German state'. *Public Administration*, 82 (3): 727–742.

Dent, M., Kirkpatrick, I. and Neogy, I. (2012) 'Medical leadership and management reform in hospitals: A comparative study'. In C. Teelken, E. Ferlie and M. Dent (eds) *Leadership in the Public Sector: Promises and Pitfalls*. London: Routledge: 105–125.

Dent, M. and Pahor, J. (2015) 'Patient involvement in Europe–a Comparative Framework'. *Journal of Health Organization and Management*, 29 (5): 546–555.

Dent, M. and Tutt, D. (2014) 'Electronic patient information systems and care pathways: The organisational challenges of implementation and integration'. *Health Informatics Journal*, 20 (3): 176–188.

De Swaan, A. (1988) *In Care of the State*. Cambridge: Polity.

DiMaggio, P. and Powell, W.W. (1991) 'The iron cage revisited: institutional isomorphism and collective rationality in organizational fields'. In W.W. Powell and P. DiMaggio (eds) *The New Institutionalism in Organizational Analysis*. Chicago and London: University of Chicago Press: 63–82.

Doolin, B. (2002) 'Enterprise discourse, professional identity and the organizational control of hospital clinicians'. *Organizational Studies*, 23 (3): 369–390.

Empson, L., Muzio, D., Broschak, J. and Hinings, B. (2015) 'Researching professional services firms: An introduction and overview'. In L. Empson, D. Muzio, D. Broschak and B. Hinings (eds) *The Oxford Handbook of Professional Services Firms*. Oxford: Oxford University Press: 1–24.

Esping-Andersen, G. (1999) *Social Foundations of Post-industrial Economics*. Cambridge: Polity Press.

Evetts, J. (2011) 'A new professionalism? Challenges and opportunities'. *Current Sociology*, 59 (4): 406–422.

Ferlie, E. and Geraghty, J. (2005) 'Professionals in public sector organizations: Implications for public sector reforming'. In E. Ferlie, L. Lynn Jnr. and C. Pollitt (eds) *The Oxford Handbook of Public Management*. Oxford: Oxford University Press: 422–425.

Fitzgerald, L., Ferlie, E., McGivern, G. and Buchanan, D. (2013) 'Distributed leadership patterns and service improvement: Evidence and argument from English healthcare'. *The Leadership Quarterly*, 24 (1): 227–239.

Freidson, E. (1985) 'The reorganization of the medical profession'. *Medical Care Review*, 42: 11–35.

Freidson, E. (1994) *Professionalism Reborn: Theory, Prophecy and Policy*. Cambridge: Policy.

Greenwood, R. and Hinings, C.R. (1993) 'Understanding strategic change: The contribution of strategic types'. *Academy of Management Journal*, 36: 1052–1081.

Greenwood, R., Hining, C.R. and Brown, J. (1990) '"P2 form" strategic management: Corporate practices in professional practices'. *Academy of Management Journal*, 33 (4): 725–755.

Greenwood, R., Hinings, C.R. and Prakash, R. (2017) '25 years of the professional partnership (P^2) form: Time to foreground its social purpose and herald the (P^3)?'. *Journal of Professions and Organization*, 4: 112–122.

Gronn, P. (2002) 'Distributed leadership as a unit of analysis'. *Leadership Quarterly*, 13 (4): 423–451.

Hansen, H.F. (2013) 'NPM in Scandinavia'. In T. Christensen and P. Laegreid (eds) *The Ashgate Research Companion to New Public Management*. Farnham: Ashgate: 113–129.

Hinings, C.R. (2016) 'Restructuring professional organizations'. In M. Dent, I.L. Bourgeault, J.-L. Denis and E. Kuhlmann (eds) *The Routledge Companion to the Professions and Professionalism*. London: Routledge: 163–174.

Hinings, C.R., Greenwood, R. and Cooper, D. (1999) 'The dynamics of change in large accounting firms'. In D. Brock, M. Powell, and C.R. Hinings (eds) *Restructuring the Professional Organization: Accounting, Healthcare and Law*. London and New York: Routledge: 131–153.

Hofstede, G. (1980) *Culture's Consequences: International Differences in Work-Related Values*. Beverley Hills, CA: Sage.

Hofstede, G. (1991) *Cultures and Organisations: The Software of the Mind*. New York: McGraw-Hill.

Hood, C. (1991) 'A public management for all seasons'. *Public Administration*, 69 (1): 3–19.

Hood, C. (1995) 'The "new public management" in the 1980s: Variations on a theme'. *Accounting, Organizations and Society*, 20 (2/3): 93–109.

House, R.J., Hanges, P., Javidan, M., Dorman, P.W. and Gupta, V. (eds) (2004) *Culture, Leadership and Organisations: The GLOBE Study of 62 Societies*. Thousand Oaks, CA: Sage.

Jespersen, P.K. and Wrede, S. (2009) 'The changing autonomy of the Nordic medical professions'. In J. Magnussen, K. Vranbaek and R.B. Saltman (eds) *Nordic Health Care Systems: Recent reforms and current policy challenges*. Maidenhead: Open University Press: 151–179.

Kirkpatrick, I. (2016) 'Hybrid management and professional leadership'. In M. Dent, I.L. Bourgeault, J.-L. Denis and E. Kuhlmann (eds) *The Routledge Companion to the Professions and Professionalism*. London: Routledge: 175–187.

Kirkpatrick, I., Ackroyd, S. and Walker, R. (2005) *The New Managerialism and Public Sector Professionalism*. Basingstoke: Palgrave Macmillan.

Kirkpatrick, I., Dent, M. and Jespersen, P. K. (2011) 'The contested terrain of hospital management: Professional projects and healthcare reforms in Denmark'. *Current Sociology*, 59 (4): 489–506.

Kirkpatrick, I., Jespersen, P. K., Dent, M. and Neogy, I. (2009) 'Medicine and management in a comparative perspective: The case of Denmark and England'. *Sociology of Health & Illness*, 11(5): 642–658.

Kirkpatrick, I., Kuhlmann, E., Hartley, K., Dent, M. and Lega, F. (2016) 'Medicine and management in European hospitals: A comparative view'. *BMC Health Services Research*, 16: 171. doi.org/10.1186/s12913-016-1388-4.

Kornberger, M., Justesen, L. and Mouritsen, J. (2011) '"When you make manager, we put a big mountain in front of you": An ethnography of managers in a Big 4 Accounting Firm'. *Accounting, Organizations and Society*, 36 (8): 514–533.

Levay, C. and Waks, C. (2009) 'Professions and the pursuit of transparency in health care: Two cases of soft autonomy'. *Organization Studies*, 30 (5): 509–527.

Llewellyn, S. (2001) '"Two-way windows": Clinicians as medical managers'. *Organizational Studies*, 22 (4): 593–623.

Martin, G.P. and Learmonth, M. (2012) 'A critical account of the rise and spread of "leadership": The case of UK healthcare'. *Social Science & Medicine*, 74: 281–288.

McDonald, R. and Harrison, S. (2004) 'The micropolitics of clinical guidelines: An empirical study'. *Policy & Politics*, 32 (2): 223–239.

Merkur, S., Mossialos, E., Long, M. and McKee, M. (2008) 'Physician revalidation in Europe'. *Clinical Medicine*, 8 (4): 371–376.

Miller, P., Kurunmäki, L. and O'leary, T. (2008) 'Accounting, hybrids and the management of risk'. *Accounting, Organizations and Society*, 33 (7–8): 942–967.

Miller, P. and Rose, N. (2008) *Governing the Present: Administering Economic, Social and Personal Life*. Cambridge: Polity.

Mintzberg, H. (1983) *Structure in Fives: Designing Effective Organizations*. Englewood Cliffs, NJ: Prentice-Hall.

Muzio, D., Aulakh, S. and Kirkpatrick, I. (2019) 'Professional occupations and organizations'. In R. Greenwood and N. Philips (eds) *Elements of Organization Theory* (Cambridge e-book series). Cambridge: Cambridge University Press.

Newman, J. (2001) *Modernising Governance: New Labour, Policy and Society*. London: Sage.

Noordegraaf, M. (2007) 'From "pure" to "hybrid" professionalism: Present-day professionalism in ambiguous public domains'. *Administration & Society*, 39 (6): 761–785.

Noordegraaf, M. (2011) 'Risky business: how professionals and professional fields (must) deal with organizational issues'. *Organizational Studies*, 32 (10): 1349–1371.

Noordegraaf, M. (2015) 'Hybrid professionalism and beyond: (New) forms of public professionalism in changing organizational and societal contexts'. *Journal of Professions and Organization*, 2: 187–206.

Noordegraaf, M. (2020) 'Protective or connective professionalism? How connected professionals can (still) act as autonomous and authoritative agents'. *Journal of Professions and Organizations*, 7 (2): 1–19.

Numerato, D., Salvatore, D. and Fattore, G. (2012) 'The impact of management on medical professionalism: A review'. *Sociology of Health & Illness*, 34 (4): 626–644.

O'Reilly, D. and Reed, M. (2011) 'The grit in the oyster: Professionalism, managerialism and leaderism as discourses of public services modernization'. *Organization Studies*, 32 (8): 1079–1101.

O'Reilly, D. and Reed, M. (2012) '"Leaderism" and the discourse of leadership in the reformation of UK public services'. In C. Teelken, E. Ferlie and M. Dent (eds) *Leadership in the Public Sector: Promises and Pitfalls*. London: Routledge: 21–43.

Peters, B.G., Pierre, J. and King, D.S. (2005) 'The politics of path dependency: Political conflict in historical institutionalism'. *The Journal of Politics*, 67 (4): 1275–1300.

Pierson, P. (1997) *Path Dependence, Increasing Returns, and the Study of Politics*. Cambridge MA: Harvard Business Center for European Studies mimeograph.

Pollitt, C. and Bouckaert, G. (2017) *Public Management Reform: A Comparative Analysis – into the Age of Austerity*. Oxford: Oxford University Press.

Powell, M.J., Brock, D.M. and Hinings, C.R. (1999) 'The changing professional organization'. In D. Brock, M. Powell and C.R. Hinings (eds) *Restructuring the Professional Organization: Accounting, Health Care and Law*. London: Routledge: 1–19.

Power, M. (1999) *The Audit Society: Rituals of Verification* (2nd edition). Oxford: Oxford University Press.

Reed, M. (2016) 'Leadership and "leaderism": The discourse of professional leadership and the practice of management control in public services'. In M. Dent, I.L. Bourgeault, J.-L. Denis and E. Kuhlmann (eds) *The Routledge Companion to the Professions and Professionalism*. London: Routledge: 200–214.

Rollings, N. (2013) 'Cracks in the post-war Keynesian settlement? The role of organised business in Britain in the rise of neo-liberalism before Margaret Thatcher'. *Twentieth Century British History*, 24 (4): 637–659.

Salter, B. (2004) *The New Politics of Medicine*. Basingstoke: Palgrave Macmillan.

Seabrook, L. (2014) 'Epistemic Arbitrage: Transnational professional knowledge in action', *Journal of Professions and Organizations*, 1: 49–64.

Tuohy, C.H. (1999) *Accidental Logics: The Dynamics of Change in the Health Care Arena in the United States, Britain and Canada*. Oxford: Oxford University Press.

Vinot, D. (2014) 'Transforming hospital management la francaise'. *International Journal of Public Sector Management*, 27 (5): 406–416.

Vinson, A.H. (2016) 'Constrained collaboration: Patient empowerment discourse as resource for countervailing power'. *Sociology of Health & Illness*, 38 (8): 1364–1378.

Von Nordenflycht, A. (2010) 'What is a professional service firm? Towards a theory and taxonomy of knowledge-intensive firms'. *Academy of Management Review*, 35 (1): 155–174.

Wilsford, D. (1994) 'Path dependency, or why history makes it difficult but not impossible to reform health care systems in a big way'. *Journal of Public Policy*, 14 (3): 251–283.

Zander, M. (1990) 'The Thatcher government's onslaught on the lawyers: Who won?'. *The International Lawyer*, 24 (3): 753–785.

6 The new professionalism

Conclusions

Whither the new professionalism?

Within this book I have made several points central to understanding the current state of the professions. First, the professions are very different to what they were in the so-called 'Golden Age' of the mid-twentieth century (Gorman and Sandefur 2011). Even the old professions of law and medicine have had to change and accept greater external regulation, accountability and management. Second, following the neo-liberal turn at the end of the twentieth century, the ecology of the professions has changed because of the challenges of market rationality to their systems of bureaucratic and occupational control. Even so, the ideal of the professions and professionalism still has a significant appeal, especially to management wishing to achieve greater productivity from their workforce (Fournier 1999). Here it reflects a particular image of professionalism, one characterised by integrity and motivation, as much as expertise, that makes the appeal to professionalism a disciplinary mechanism rather than an attribute of expert labour organised as professions. Today the professions are no longer the predominantly autonomous, male-dominated, self-regulating domains they once were. The professions have been reconfigured and the notion of professionalism has been reconceptualised. These changes have largely been associated with the rise of neo-liberalism although other factors have also had an impact, social movements as a key example, have left their mark, notably in relation to gender and racial equality; although, this is still unfinished business. While there are national variations overall, there are discernible commonalities as to how all these factors have reconfigured the professions. This has included the increasing stratification of professional workforces within the large public sector and corporate organisations, which may well reduce the prospects of junior members to achieve senior positions or partnerships. This is coupled with the growth in the use of protocols and guidelines which now govern much professional work. To stay with the latter, protocols and guidelines, for a moment, as they are particularly interesting in relation to the shaping of the work and governance of the professions. They are to be found within law, nursing, medicine, accountancy,

DOI: 10.4324/9780429430831-6

consultancy and elsewhere. While these would appear to be systems of control (and they are to a degree) they are constructed and maintained by the professions themselves. They are largely the responsibility of the more senior members of the professions, or special working groups brought together for the purpose. This means that these professions, corporately rather than individualistically, continue to display all the expertise and influence associated with autonomous professions. This is so, even if at the same time the work of many within the professions has become substantially routinised. Integral to this general development we have seen professionals taking on managerial roles as part of their responsibilities. The professions are still with us, although somewhat different than they were only a few decades ago.

To have survived as well as they have the professions have found it necessary to negotiate revised jurisdictions for themselves. No longer are they able to claim, let alone enjoy, unquestioned rights to autonomy and self-regulation, for these principles have come under much critical scrutiny, a lot of it couched in the language of trust and risk. This decline of trust in the expertise or professionalism of professionals has happened in part because, from time to time, certain professionals demonstrate they cannot be trusted and can even be very dangerous (as, for example, in the UK case of Dr. Shipman, the murdering doctor, discussed in Chapter 4). But more mundanely and largely due to the rise in the widespread use of the world wide web, professionals are no longer believed to have the monopoly of expert knowledge. Moreover, it is often assumed that the layperson has, potentially, a good understanding of the uncertainty and risks involved, something that was not the case previously (Brown and Calnan 2016). Even when that is not the case, the clients tend to prefer to have professionals held to account by an official agency on their behalf. A relevant example that is in the news as I am writing this relates to Ofsted (Office for Standards in Education) in England. Many parents rely on Ofsted reports to decide what school they want to send their children to. However, in this particular instance, its inspectors had awarded a particular primary school in the south of England a much worse rating than it had a few years previously. As a consequence, as it has been reported in the media, the headteacher committed suicide. On this tragic occasion, the agency (Ofsted) with responsibility for monitoring quality and standards came under sharp critical scrutiny by the media and public. Clearly, there is a tension here that cannot be easily resolved. More usually the discomfort of a critical external scrutiny is solely one experienced by the professionals, for as McDonald and Spence (2016: 103) have observed:

> [w]e have witnessed a shift away from trusting professionals towards holding them to account against measurable criteria.

This has been the consequence of the neo-liberal project of the 1980s and later that also saw an imposition of management on the professions, especially (but not only) within the public sector, that led to the emergence of the hybrid professional, who combined both professional and managerial responsibilities. These 'boundary spanners' had to be credible to their professional colleagues to be effective, whilst advising management as managers. Over time, these various 'hybrid' roles have become normalised within the professions and their work organisations and the narrative has changed from managerialism to leadership. To begin with, there was considerable cynicism around the narrative, some seeing it as a manipulative rhetoric that has been labelled 'leaderism' (Reed 2016; O'Reilly and Reed 2012), but over time it has begun to coalesce into a set of practices that provide professionals with a basis for a new form of work-based autonomy, one that incorporates the realities of the financial 'bottom line', some form of performance management and quality control/improvement function. The example given in Chapter 5 was that of the nurse leadership in the development of integrated care pathways, which can cause inter-professional tensions with their medical colleagues. Other examples would include the expectation that professional leaders need to be entrepreneurial in the pursuit of new business for their schools, hospitals or other public sector agencies as much as their law and accountancy colleagues in the private sector. This entrepreneurial tendency is not the only trend discernible in the evolution of the professions, in addition to the market rationale there are the community networks premised on trust and reported on by Adler and Kwon (2008) all reflecting the ability of professions to evolve and innovate in their responses to the pressures and messages from others in their actor-networks.

On the issue of client or user involvement, whose roots, in part, were in political philosophy (Dryzek 2000) and political activism (Arnstein 1969) – although the consumerist element of user involvement does not share this tradition, being more a product of the marketisation of public services. The implementation of user involvement – and consumerism – can be viewed, initially at least, as an attempt to strengthen managerial authority vis-à-vis professionals (Dent and Pahor 2015). For the professional's performance can be measured relative to the user/consumer's assessment, which would seem to have provided management with a useful tool to manage the professionals. However, in the case of medicine, for example, we have seen the profession reversing that tendency and increasingly co-opting and incorporating their users and clients for their own agendas. This is where the lexicon changes from user involvement changes to co-production. More broadly, Noordegraaf (2015, 2020) has extended the argument, asserting that what we are now witnessing is a move from the traditional 'protective' mode of professionalism to a more 'connective' one. Professions, in varying ways, increasingly press to co-produce their services with management, service users, government agencies and others in order that they institutionally retain a leadership role in determining the continued centrality of their services and its direction of travel. How this trend develops will vary, dependent on the local histories (pathway dependencies) as well as the challenges and opportunities that confront them.

It would be premature, however, to suggest that the professions have given up on traditional methods of jurisdictional control, for as critics of Noordegraaf's (2020) paper have made clear, the traditional 'protective' mode of professionalism is still a significant force among the organised professions. Even so, given the social and organisational changes that have occurred since the arrival of neo-liberalism, the 'connective' mode does provide a good basis for future research. So too are those other forms of professionalism that have grown outside the protective model. I am thinking here of the entrepreneurial professions (Reed 1996) working, for example, in computing, information technologies and media. Also, the emerging, or neo-professions – the knowledge workers – who staff the Professional Services Firms (PSFs) (Muzio, Ackroyd and Chanlat 2008) the accountants, lawyers and others with more established claims to institutionalised professional status.

Conclusion

The professions and professionalism have been changing, principally the result of the decline of the twentieth-century welfare state arrangements that had so influenced the modern theorising of the professions. In their previous forms, the professions depended on their historically and variously constructed jurisdictions (social closure), which fitted the political and social needs of the welfare state. In the wake of the shift to neo-liberalism in the West in the later quarter of the twentieth century, much, if not all, of this has changed. Today the professions have had to negotiate revised jurisdictions and, in the process, accept a greater role for external regulation and the involvement of lay members on their professional councils and association boards. At the same time, and for similar reasons, Western governments, corporations along with users and consumers continue to be faced by a changing and uncertain world and therefore continue to feel the need for access to expert labour (professionals). It is within this reality that the professions have adapted and are adapting. This newer world of professions and professionalism is one that is less concerned with the pursuit of social closure and more with performativity (Dent and Whitehead 2002: 8) coupled with an emphasis on professional identity and a claim to an expertise based on – and validated by – specialist knowledge and expertise commonly coupled with market demand.

Professions, like the British monarchy, appear to have always been with us, yet like the monarchy they have had to adapt and change over time to survive and even to thrive. In the last 50 years, however, the organised professions have experienced particularly intense pressures to change the ways they are organised, governed and even justify their very existence. How the professions have responded to these challenges has been the subject of this short book leading to the ambivalent conclusion – echoing the monarchy – 'the professions (as we have known them) are dead, long live the professions!'.

References

All internet links accessed and checked on 24 May 2023 or later

Adler, P.S., and Kwon, S.-W. (2008) 'Community, market and hierarchy in the evolving organization of professional work: The case of medicine'. In D. Muzio, S. Ackroyd and J.-F. Chanlat (eds) *Redirections in the Study of Expert Labour: Established Professions and New Expert Occupations*. Basingstoke: Palgrave Macmillan: 139–160.

Arnstein, S.R. (1969) 'A ladder of citizen participation'. *Journal of American Institute of Planners*, 35 (3): 216–224.

Brown, P. and Calnan, M. (2016) 'Professional, trust and cooperation'. In M. Dent, I.L. Bourgeault, J.-L. Denis and E. Kuhlmann (eds) *The Routledge Companion to the Professions and Professionalism*. London: Routledge: 129–143.

Dent, M. and Pahor, J. (2015) 'Patient involvement in Europe–a comparative framework'. *Journal of Health Organization and Management*, 29 (5): 546–555.

Dent, M. and Whitehead, S. (2002) 'Configuring the "new professional"'. In M. Dent and S. Whitehead (eds) *Managing Professional Identities: Knowledge, Performativity and the 'New' Professional*. London: Routledge: 1–16.

Dryzek, J.S. (2000) *Deliberative Democracy and Beyond: Liberals, Critics, Contestations*. Oxford: Oxford University Press.

Fournier, V. (1999) 'The appeal of "professionalism" as a disciplinary mechanism'. *The Sociological Review*, 47 (2): 280–307.

Gorman, E.H. and Sandefur, R.L. (2011) '"Golden Age," quiescence, and revival: How the sociology of professions became the study of knowledge-based work'. *Work and Occupations*, 38 (3): 275–302.

Johnson, T. (1972) *Professions and Power*. London: Macmillan.

McDonald, R. and Spence, C. (2016) 'Professions and financial incentives'. In M. Dent, I.L. Bourgeault, J.-L. Denis and E. Kuhlmann (eds) *The Routledge Companion to the Professions and Professionalism*. London: Routledge: 102–115.

Muzio, D., Ackroyd, S., and Chanlat, J.-F. (2008) 'Introduction: lawyers, doctors and business consultants'. In D. Muzio, S. Ackroyd and J.-F. Chanlat (eds) *Redirections in the Study of Expert Labour*. Basingstoke: Palgrave: 1–28.

Noordegraaf, M. (2015) 'Hybrid professionalism and beyond: (New) forms of public professionalism in changing organizational and societal contexts'. *Journal of Professions and Organization*, 2: 187–206.

Noordegraaf, M. (2020) 'Protective or connective professionalism? How connected professionals can (still) act as autonomous and authoritative agents'. *Journal of Professions and Organizations*, 7 (2):1–19

O'Reilly, D., and Reid, M. (2012) '"Leaderism" and the discourse of leadership in the reformation of UK public services'. In C. Teelken, E. Ferlie and M. Dent (eds) *Leadership in the Public Sector: Promises and pitfalls*. London: Routledge: 21–43.

Reed, M. (1996) 'Expert power and control in late modernity: An empirical review and theoretical synthesis'. *Organization Studies*, 17 (4): 573–597.

Reed, M. (2016) 'Leadership and "leaderism": the discourse of professional leadership and the practice of management control in public services'. In M. Dent, I.L. Bourgeault, J-L Denis and E. Kuhlmann (eds) *The Routledge Companion to the Professions and Professionalism*. London: Routledge: 200–214.

Index

For Product Safety Concerns and Information please contact our EU
representative GPSR@taylorandfrancis.com
Taylor & Francis Verlag GmbH, Kaufingerstraße 24, 80331 München, Germany

www.ingramcontent.com/pod-product-compliance
Ingram Content Group UK Ltd.
Pitfield, Milton Keynes, MK11 3LW, UK
UKHW021501240926
475702UK00035B/89

* 9 7 8 1 1 3 8 3 6 5 2 1 6 *